THE SIGN OF THE SWORD

**SHAYKH
'ABDALQADIR
AL-MURABIT**

© Shaykh Abdalqadir al-Murabit
Murabitun Publications
P.O. Box 436
Norwich NR3 1LL
First printed in 1984

Ayat as-Sayf

"So, when you meet the kuffar strike at their necks: at length, when you have thoroughly controlled them, tie them up firmly; after that, either generosity or ransom, until the war lays down its burdens. Thus (do it): but if it had been Allah's will, He could certainly have (Himself) taken retribution from them; but (He lets you fight) in order to test you, some with others.

But those who are killed in the Way of Allah - He will never let their actions be lost."

INTRODUCTION	i
THE ENEMY	13
JIHAD	26
Six Conditions of Jihad	37
Six Rules of Jihad	38
Jihad against Three Groups	40
FIVE ELEMENTS OF JIHAD	44
Al-Jizya wa'dh-Dhimma	48
Ghazwat	60
Al-Ghanima wa'l-'Abeed	68
JIHAD - FURTHER PRINCIPLES	85
THE AYAT OF THE SWORD	96

Preface to 1991 Edition

In the time since this work was written the basic argument it contains has been confirmed by history. It is now clear that the forces of kufr are one force, not two in dialectical opposition. It is now obvious that the instrument by which the new world order, that is, rule by the unelected banking elite, intends to control mankind is constitutional democracy. There was a moment when it seemed that Iran had taken on the task of defending Islam, but the two necessary conditions were never met: the abolition of state control to be replaced by empowered government, and the abolition of a haram money system and haram participation in the world banking hegemony.

There was no way I could have imagined, when this work was written, the ferocious attacks that would be carried out against me and my work for Islam by the Saudi regime and its satellites. When we held a conference of Maliki Fiqh in Abu Dhabi, the head of the Emirates, Shaykh Zayed turned up at one session and declared before the assembled 'ulama' that he confirmed that he would rule by the Book and the Sunna. We all dutifully applauded, but our people noted that the hotel in Abu Dhabi where some of us had been housed was in fact a brothel - owned by Shaykh Zayed's Minister of Islamic Affairs. Now such personal wrong action is obliterated before the shameful crime of handing over the Arabian peninsula to the military might of jewish America.

The decadence of the Emirates, and the sadly compromised nature of the resident Ikhwan there, was nothing, however, to the shameless scandal of the degenerate Saudi regime. Fahd, groomed and monitored from the beginning as the puppet of jewish-american investment, is himself beneath contempt. Yet more dismal in human terms are the helplessly compromised leaders of the so-called Salafi movement who operate out of Riyadh. They are all disgraced. Now the dynamic and purified elements of the Ikhwan at last are heard. The Muslims are united and the affair has just begun.

It is vital at this stage that two traps are avoided. One is the surrender to a worker-generous socialism which veils its true intent to create another western model in place of defunct monarchism. The other is the failure to grasp that the controlling function in the kafir system is the world-networked usury system of banks and stock-exchange control. It is this cancer against which the true Jihad has to be waged. The Intifada has become globalised. Yet, at the same time, we cannot continue the forbidden practice of allowing children who have not reached puberty to do our fighting for us. Probably by the time this goes into print Yasser Arafat will have been swept away. We will long remember his disgraceful salutations to the zionist intriguer, Bruno Kreiski, at the latter's funeral.

For Jihad, the banner of Islam must be raised high. We must act *fi sabil-illah*.

Allah unite us in the noble struggle.
La ghaliba illa'llah.

Shaykh Abdalqadir As-Sufi Al-Murabit

This is a textbook on matters pertaining to the Deen of Islam in accordance with the Book of Allah and the Sunna of His Messenger, may Allah bless him and grant him peace. In the matters discussed the position taken is based firmly on the view of these two primal sources, and, in accordance with the orders of the Messenger, may Allah bless him and grant him peace, we draw also on the practice of the Salaf, being the first three generations, with particular respect to the rightly-guided Khalifs.

In this time we find that the Deen, this original prophetic matter has been virtually rewritten by Egyptian and Pakistani journalists claiming to be the leaders of a modernist 'revival'. During the period of their influence and programme the Muslims have been more and more degraded, led astray, trapped into paramilitary actions without a rational possibility of success, forced to accept a doctrine which tolerated kafir banking while pretending it eliminated the very usury which lay at the source of all the Muslims' miseries. At the same time these alleged 'leaders' have either been killed in naive adventures and then exalted almost as gods above criticism, or installed as the governors of those same haram banks made rich by the small savings of the poor Muslims.

'Ulama' in the pay of governments given over to programmes which are openly committed to the deen of kufr and allied to Islam's deadly enemies have held conferences and made pronouncements, even official fatwas, consenting to the rewriting of the Deen - to the alteration of the rites of Hajj, and to the denial of clear ayats on the duties of both

Zakat and Jihad.

If a country has made itself the host to kafir military installations, how can anyone seriously consider that country's scholars worthy of the name, or capable of ijtihad, indeed even capable of issuing the most fundamental order, when on that simple issue their lips are sealed? When Islamic education has been traduced, rewritten, and rendered inactive, submitted to the academic system of the kuffar which by its declared methodology considers every text to be a created one subject to critique analysis and rejection, thus openly denying the Qur'an's Divine nature; when genuine 'ulama' are refused a voice while kafir manufactured 'doctors', who have openly and eagerly submitted to the university system's accolades of approval and membership into the kafir deen, speak out. It is out of these same universities that the so-called 'doctors' have emerged with their syncretist Islam that utterly accepts the foundations of the kafir system, its structuralism, its masonism, its secularism, its jewish science and sociology, its jewish psychiatry which already is installed in the Arab lands, and worst of all, its brilliantly redesigned 'modern Islam' which tells the gullible that Islam did not spread by the sword but by rational argument - although how the invading Arabs were able to persuade Spanish, Chinese, Malay, and Berber hordes of Islamic superiority when they did not speak their languages remains a secret.

Now we have had a good hundred years since the masonic works of 'Abdu and his cohorts have laid waste to the Islamic heartland. The so-called Islamic

Movement, so cleverly claiming to be Salafi, while initiating bid'a after bid'a has conducted uprisings over the last fifty years not one of which has succeeded. Indeed, critics have noted how often their activities suited the British or American foreign policies of the time. Thousands of young men have been slaughtered and never once has the victory, most certainly assured the Muslims when the banner of Islam is raised high, come to pass. Once a messenger came to 'Umar ibn al-Khattab with news of a Muslim victory and 'Umar asked him, "At what time did you engage the enemy?" He replied, "In the early morning." Then he was asked, "At what time were they defeated?" He replied, "Shortly after noon." 'Umar exclaimed, "We belong to Allah and to Him shall we return! Did kufr stand up to Iman from early morning until midday? You have made a bid'a behind my back!"

So what are we to make of a school and an ijtihad that has failed so abominably for fifty years, while at present all its founding members bask in the luxury of serving the very enemy who now enslaves our millions from Indonesia to Africa?

What are we to make of a so-called Islamic leadership that takes all its social structures and patterns of behaviour from the kuffar? For not only are 'academic' credentials, not spiritual ones, required of the 'ulama', but the social mores of ministries, ambassadors, protocols, national Academies and other such fantasies are treated with the greatest awe both at the national and the international level. To such a degree have some Muslim nations grovelled before kafir behaviour, they even allow their reputation for drinking and smoking and party-giving, whose natural outcome is fornication and adultery, to be a subject of boasting and reputation. The Arab at the race-course gambling, at the Casino gambling, and in the night-club is not only a common and familiar figure, but his friendship with the worst elements of the kuffar is nothing less than his adulation of the jewish enemy against which he claims such animosity.

However, much worse than this personal immorality is the social and business ethos which places him in the board-room of the multi-national corporation and the mega-bank face to face with the jewish enemy underwriting the very economy which dooms the Arab peoples and the Muslim heartland to its continued slavery.

Allah the Exalted clearly states in His Book:

> O you who believe, take not the jews and the Christians for your friends and protectors: they are only friends and protectors to each other. And he among you that turns to them is of them. Truly Allah guides not an unjust people. (5: 54)

He, exalted is He, also says:

> The kafirun are protectors one of another; unless you do this (protect each other) there will be corruption and oppression on the

> earth, and great trouble. 'Those who believe and make hijra and fight in the way of Allah as well as those who give asylum and aid - these are the true believers; for them is the forgiveness of wrong actions and a provision most generous. (8: 74-5)

But this befriending is not something special to the power elite and the military and business communities. It is shared by the common people in hundreds of distressing ways from the dress of the kuffar, and the resultant sustaining of the absurd fashion industry of the jews, to the games they play and their shameless dress exposing human bodies for sport, to the films and the television which are produced and scripted openly by jews insulting the religion of Islam and the very person of our noble Messenger, may Allah bless him and grant him peace, and calling people to sexual immorality and the abandoning of what is halal for what is haram. When the French installed a French-language TV-channel with deliberately immoral and kafir programmes into Tunisia, where was the protest? Why were the cables not destroyed, the transmitting station obliterated? But the question must be asked right across the Arab world. And since when has the matter been one of purely private morality? We must come quickly to the real issue which is social. It is the matter of banking, and of hosting kafir militarism, for it is the taking of friends among the kuffar at the level of weaponry and monetary system and education that has destroyed the Islamic ethos so effectively and cleverly in the last hundred years. Young people now read an Islam which they think engages the issues of fighting the kuffar, when the leadership of the movement itself is funded by these very forces they think they are opposing - a secret society Islam whose leadership is hidden and whose funding is from the enemy, a youth movement and a student movement whose mores are based on the Christian fascist movements and whose sole job is to discover future activists and then recruit them into the state apparatus of their countries or into the new 'official Islam' with its ludicrous Ministries of Islamic Affairs. What constitutes an Islamic affair? Should we not ask: what affair is not an Islamic one?

> Your friend is only Allah and His Messenger and those who believe, who perform the prayer and pay the zakat, and bow down. And whoever takes Allah and His Messenger and those who believe for friends - indeed, the party of Allah, they are the victorious (5: 58-59)

'Abdullah ibn 'Umar said: 'He who settles in the land of the mushrikun, celebrates their holidays and festivals, and imitates them throughout his life will be raised along with them on the Day of Rising.'

Abu Dawud in his *Sunan* relates that the Messenger, may Allah bless him and grant him peace, said: 'He who imitates a people belongs to them.'

> O you who believe, take not the kafirun as friends in preference to the believers. Do you wish to

> give Allah an open proof against yourselves? (4: 144)

As-Suyuti says this means a clear proof of your hypocrisy.

Allah, exalted is He, also says:

> O you who believe! do not take My enemy and your enemies as friends. Would you offer them love even though they have rejected the Truth that has come to you? (60: 1)

There is no doubt that the Muslim umma has been seduced, tricked and subverted into a disastrous friendship with the kuffar, the result of which has been the abandonment of our educational nexus for theirs, our moral nexus for theirs, our governmental nexus for their, our judiciary nexus for theirs, so that our anthropological distinctness has been submerged and eradicated, until all that is allowed to remain is a romantic appraisal of our 'Islamic' past in Museums of Mankind and other jew-designed mortuaries of wisdom and life that once belonged to other peoples presently made slaves to their usurious society.

Ashamed of our defeat at the hands of the enemy, we submitted to the deen of kufr vainly imagining there could be an Islamic society based on kafir principles and mores. The repellent and utterly disastrous modernist movement, with its rewritten Islam cleared by the enemy as a no-risk version of the militant and victorious Islam they had once so feared, managed to sell to the Arab world and the Muslim heartland an Islam devoid of the essential elements on which its life depended.

At the first sign of Islamic revival the kafir forces howled about fundamentalism and 'going back fourteen hundred years' and turning the back on progress. The truth is their society is a total failure, morally, spiritually and politically. It is a record of horror, torture, human degradation and death unparalleled in the history of man. According to World Health Organisation statistics - about which the same vast organisation is helpless - 900 million people are suffering from famine. In the poor countries 30 children die every minute, that is, one child dies every two seconds. Is this what we have to remain silent about - their brave new world?

Allah, glory be to Him, says in His Book:

> And when We desire to destroy a city, We send a command to its men who live at ease, and after it they commit wrong actions, so that the word is proved true against them, then We destroy them utterly. (17: 16)

The arrogant wealth of usurious bankers has not created a compassionate society. This so-called scientific basis of modern society far from being humanitarian has proved worse than the worst excesses of the jahilivya. While the Chinese pretend to be 'modern' and institute birth-control laws against what Allah and His Messenger, may Allah bless him and grant him peace, have decreed by Book and Sunna, they find themselves in the same morally bankrupt and pagan position that was their ancestors'. With these limited families, the Chinese by tradition desire a son; faced with these unjust rules the parents have been driven to the murder of newborn girls - exactly what the Messenger was sent to put an end to fourteen hundred years ago.

Allah the Exalted declares:

> When the female (child) buried alive is questioned - for what crime she was killed - when the pages are laid open - when the heaven is unveiled - when the Blazing Fire is burning fiercely - and when the Garden is brought near - then every self will know what it has put forward. (81: 8-14)

Declaring 'Liberty, fraternity and equality', the masonic ethos of jew-controlled Christian society has enslaved the muslims, treated them like dogs and degraded them and the Deen of Islam. The Arab, the keystone of our intellectual life, has been massacred in waves of genocide, his lands used as a killing ground for kafir wars, his wealth stolen from him and worthless paper money put in its place. His lands are occupied by kafir forces for his 'protection' against other kuffar. He has had puppets placed over him against his will. A false 'Islamic Movement' has been foisted on him inviting the activist to undertake the suicide mission so that he can in turn be identified and slaughtered. The brilliant satanic dialectic has, in under one hundred years, rendered us all helpless. Now, surrounded by the haram and the humanly disgusting lifestyle of kufr, we are asked to be good Muslims, get into business, put our money in Islamic banks, and submit to the internationalist hegemony run by jews with no more interest in Israel than the Eskimoes, for it has never been anything but a militant distraction to keep the Arabs occupied while the real crime, the banking hegemony, was thrown over the Arab nation and the Muslims, netting them and imprisoning them in the magic of abstract, zero-worth, paper money.

It is, in short, time to identify the enemy and declare the Jihad. It is time to finish with an emasculated Islam voided of its *fara'id* (obligations) and the necessary conditions without which it cannot win and it cannot survive. It is time to restore the Book and the Sunna to their sublime position of uncompromising success and take the promised victory assured to us by Allah.

Identify the enemy. Declare the Jihad. Define its parameters. Indicate its opening stages. Delineate its outcome and indicate its end.

And our prayer is: Allah return us to the Guiding Book and the Helping Sword. Amin.

THE ENEMY

In locating the enemy we must immediately be aware that it is not a nation with a politique and an army and a flag - although they can send armies into the field. It is not a nation - it is in fact 'international' yet it will invoke the legitimacy of national laws and rights to defend its non-nation based power. Floating a haram paper (promissory) money they themselves are ensconced in a power situation of gold reserve, gold market 'price' manipulation, the diamond market and other fall-back systems of 'real wealth' in the deliberately orchestrated phases of inflation and bankruptcy.

> Yahya related to me from Malik from Musa ibn Abi Tamim from Abu'l-Hubab Sa'id ibn Yasar from Abu Hurayra that the Messenger of Allah, may Allah bless him and grant him peace, said, "A dinar for a dinar, a dirham for a dirham, no excess between the two." (*Al-Muwatta'*, 31.16.29)

That the real human transactional business ethos of Madinan Islam remains on record is a miracle of the miracles of the Messenger of Allah, may Allah bless him and grant him peace. The contrast between its social justice and the gross gigantism of billion dollar debts and the macabre trillions of dollar debt the people of the United States owe to private banking underlines both the deep humanism and sanity of Islam and the demented nature of the usurious society. It is clear, however, that there is no road of reformism possible for their society. There has been a slow erosion of realism from the days of Thomas Jefferson and the banking crises, whose culmination was the cataclysmic upheaval of two European wars, each based on the irrational malfunction of the monetary system which had no basis in real wealth, gold and silver.

> Malik related to me that Zayd ibn Aslam said, "Usury in the Jahiliyya was that a man would give a loan to a man for a set term. When the term was due, he would say, 'Will you pay it off or increase me?' If the man paid, he took it. If not, he increased him in his debt and lengthened it for him."
>
> Malik said, "The disapproved way of doing things, about which there is no dispute among us, is that a man gives a loan to a man for a term, and then the demander reduces it, and the one from whom it is demanded pays it in advance. To us that is like someone who delays repaying his debt after it is due to his creditor and his creditor increases his debt."
>
> Malik said, "This is nothing else but usury. No doubt about it."
> (*Al-Muwatta'*, 31.39.83)

The jews and their Christian cohorts knew that they had one final act before the complete subversion of Islam to kufr. They had dismantled the legal systems which were the social purpose of Islam. They had made contradictory arguments both accepting the madh-habs and rejecting them as causing conflict among the Muslims - while nowhere on the political horizon could be seen a unified 'school' - it was a theoretical fantasy which they well knew would never be, and would in any event be nothing other than a fifth madh-hab. They had supplanted the great tafsir literature with modernist journalism which nowhere laid bare the necessary *ahkam* (rulings) which lead to legal judgement and political action. They had allowed a rhetoric of Jihad while destroying it as a realistic programme since, as we will see, *insha'llah*, they had denied its fundamental rules. The final act was to bring the whole Muslim nation into the realm of riba and haram banking while cynically convincing the common people that it was 'Islamic' banking - when the word itself means usury and is not an Arabic word. Within ten short years we were to see the leaders of the modernist movement established in wealth at the head of the so-called 'Islamic Banking' nexus.

There is no need to pretend to theoretical discussion on the issue in the way that modernist literature, which now abounds, has done, demonstrating by 'economic theory' that their system is not usurious. The inescapable fact is that banking by its nature is one global system. If you plug into it with one small 'clean' investment called non-interest banking it still must interface throughout the whole larger system until it becomes immediately and automatically enmeshed in the usurious process. One single credit facility to a country can involve up to over one hundred banks in the process and entangle capital flow in a multitude of usurious investments. Yet the passive involvement of 'Islamic banking' in the usurious system is not where the matter ends. Already there is clear evidence that its ventures are geared to the abolition of Islamic education and knowledge. Funding from 'Islamic' banks has gone to support kafir universities and even the building of churches. So-called 'Islamic banking', far from being a solution to the danger of usury, is the deliberate deception of the people by the usurious enemy who have subverted the munafiqun to their purpose of illegal gain.

> Malik related to me that he heard that 'Abdullah ibn Mas'ud used to say, "if someone makes a loan, they should not stipulate better than it. Even if it is a handful of grass, it is usury." (*Al-Muwatta'*, 31.44.95)

Another deliberate over-simplification of the kafir banking system is that banking operates in some kind of economic vacuum. While it has its own rules and systems, it is utterly interactive with other networked institutions of the mushrik anthropology. Banking is wed to the Stock Exchange system which is both its ally and its enemy. Clustered around that system are the whole body of commodity markets and futures markets, even penny markets for the poor investors. The Arab nation has already experienced the magical power of market manipulation of the spot markets and stock exchanges. At one moment they held a political power by their control of the price of oil. It took only just over a year for the enemy to re-align the value of the same commodity until it was devalued to the point that these same oil nations have been taken to the edge of bankruptcy.

What is presented to the people as a kind of self-operating Minotaur that cannot be predicted - the Crash of '29, and so on - in reality is orchestrated with a Mozartian finesse and mathematical precision. It is quite amazing how the munafiqun, who wished to enmesh the Muslim nation in banking, were able to avoid the fact that this meant total immersion in the stock exchange system, with its futures market and other practices so clearly and unmistakably forbidden in the Book of Allah and in the Sunna of the Messenger, may Allah grant him blessings and peace.

We have no choice but to characterise the whole monetary system as usurious. That is to say the interactive networked system of banks and megabanks (IMF, World Bank, etc), stock exchanges and all forms of trading conducted under their protocols, are nothing other than the true face of usurious power control which openly governs the world through its own organisations and personnel. They, in turn, are dispersed over the banking system as such, and are interlocked with the vassal systems of so-called democratic governments and their agencies on the one hand, and the puppet dictators who rule the debtor client nations on the other.

All this can be identified rationally and openly without recourse to conspiracy theory or arcane identification of secret masonic societies and so on, although these bizarre elements serve the so-called rationality of the main system as has been repeatedly demonstrated in recent history, as in the scandals surrounding the catholic church and the Mafia and the masonic control systems that ran the Italian government (and in a new form still does).

The weave of modern society crosses and double crosses from the economic and business world to the political, and the political world simply provides the theatrical arena for the masses to personalise the issues as a series of party and individual crises and interactions, veiling the true nature of the issues which never cease to involve money and its activities in banking, borrowing, and the taking over of real power by its method, that is gold, silver, ownership of production and land. Bankruptcy, for a bank, is a means of access to the private wealth of ordinary people and indeed even the wealthy of the pre-banking regime.

'International' banking is a system without any national allegiance or institutionalised central authority. Parasitic as usury is, it lives off and uses the existing national and international agencies of politics and economics, as well as its own multi-faced public identity as high-street bank, national bank, state bank, conglomerate, mega-bank and world power institution. And all this in turn is utterly enmeshed with the multi-national corporate and the supranational methods of corporation activity which removes these mega-structures from so-called national political and economical control. Indeed, nationalism has been an aesthetic and nothing more since the Bretton Woods Agreement.

Nor should there be any illusion that this is a 'capitalist' philosophy. In the East we are merely dealing with state-banking and a different design pattern to the same acquiescence to the banking masters. The vodka-cola syndrome has long since revealed the indistinguishable nature of the modern monetary control system. That the Chase Manhattan has a branch in Moscow, address, 1, Karl Marx Square, does not mean they are communist agents but rather reveals that the east/west dialectic is merely a method of vitalising trade wars and capital competition.

Sophisticated arguments in the language of 'economic theory' are scripted by jewish economists in their intellectual strongholds, those same universities which have taken command of 'Islamic studies', so that within the short span of ten years they have made the Muslim governments demand academic credentials as a proof of Islamic knowledge, when it is not merely a proof of ignorance but a badge of being the enemy's agent. The Islamic *'duktur'* - another non-Arabic signifier - is himself the apologist of an Islam without power to fight.

The banking system is, in detail and in general, a usury edifice with a usurious central principle and with usury its necessary condition. On the matter, the Qur'an is uncompromising.

Allah, glory be to Him, says:

Those who devour usury will not stand except as stands one whom Shaytan by his touch has driven to madness. That is because they say: trade is like usury. But Allah has permitted trade and forbidden usury. Those, who after receiving direction from their Lord desist, shall be pardoned for the past: their case is for Allah. But those who repeat are Companions of the Fire: they will remain there. Allah will deprive usury of all blessing, but will give increase for deeds of sadaqa: for He loves not creatures ungrateful and bad.

Those who believe and do deeds of goodness and establish prayer and pay the zakat will have their reward with their Lord: there shall be no fear on them nor shall they sorrow.

O you who believe, fear Allah and give up what remains of your demand for usury, if you are indeed believers.

If you do it not, take notice of war from Allah and His Messenger.

But if you turn back you shall have your capital sums: deal not unjustly and you shall not be dealt with unjustly. (2: 275-279)

This is a clear declaration of war by Allah and His Messenger. That is, by Divine Decree and the laws of Islam, where usury is practised is Dar al-Harb and a zone for Jihad under Divine and prophetic authorisation. Small wonder the *'dukturs'* have declared that the concept of Dar al-Harb and Dar al-Islam are no longer valid in this age. On the contrary - we find that it is the terrain of international banking that is the arena of usury, and so is Dar al-Harb, until the victory, the inevitable and promised victory of the forces of Islam.

Significantly, in the light of this great ayat we observe how the Muslims, especially in the Arab heartland of the Umma were led astray by the modernist and revisionist 'ulama'. Absorbing the language and methodology of kufr in preference to the Islamic language and method, they found themselves thinking and acting not like muslims but rather like either reactionary rightists with political ambitions in the arena of assembly politics or radicals with fantasies of revolution. Of course, revolution is a rabbinical invention whose model is the anti-religious French revolution which was put in place by the encyclopaedists, the precursors of the new jewish elites of Harvard and MIT. Islam can no more absorb the foreign concepts of revolution and socialism than it can the equally alien ideas of interest-based loans and zero-worth money disconnected from bi-metal wealth in the hand.

It is not an accident that the result of one hundred years of redefining Islam meant that its only means to militant action should be couched in the masonic model of a secret society of Assassins, and this not for the first time in Islam's history. One of the major tragedies resulting from this strategy, quite apart from the slaughter of muslim youth without ever a victory, in open defiance of the clear laws of Jihad known to those 'ulama' who still had access to the primal material, was that Muslims adopted a naive western political view which was strictly based on personality politics.

The idea that a society controlled by an all-embracing web of networked banking and supranational control systems could yield to the assassination of a President here and a Prime Minister there was a proof of ignorance of the enemy and an abandonment of the Book of guidance and the model of the Sunna.

In the scenario of modern kufr, the role of politicians - who exert no more than a personal style - is precisely to act as centre stage actors drawing the attention of the masses from the theft of wealth and resources going on on the sidelines. The assassination of one American president and the disgracing of another made scarcely a ripple on the market nor an indentation on the value of the dollar.

Once politics has been identified as a snare to trap would-be activists against the kafir, it follows that the mythic vocabulary of national entities be recognised. National sovereignty, like political power, is a pseudo-authority to control the masses. Flags are for sports arenas and local parades. Their reality is purely propagandist and rhetorical. Once the banking entity has injected its blood into the body politic, it is no longer a discrete entity but rather an amorphous mass without legal boundaries. Governments merely initiate massive loans, and must be removed if they hinder debt repayment or rescheduling. On the whole there are benign 'democracies' for the arena of the dominant banking forces and puppet dictatorships for the poor countries, who must continue to hand over their raw materials and commodity wealth in exchange for debt enslavement. Sometimes a 'revolutionary movement' is necessary to reduce the population to controllable levels by genocide and also to try out new weaponry designed by the banking entities.

It is vital that the Muslim mujahideen do not mistake the enemy and think this is a war against a nation or leader. Although the struggle may present leaders and nations to distract and ensnare the Islamic forces, it is Jihad - under orders from Allah and His Messenger, may Allah bless him and grant him peace. It is a Jihad against the usurious banking entity. Thus it is a struggle that can be waged not just on one terrain, or under one Amir, but it is Jihad that will be characterised by fighting wherever the enemy's forces exist.

The enemy is not merely a personnel but a method, a deen, with its Temples, the banks; with its holy places, the Stock Exchanges of the world; and its false scriptures, the data-banks of figures, these magical millions and billions that hold the world's poor to ransom for the sake of a small elite of kafir power brokers, their core jewish, their allies the lawless Christians. It is with these that war must be waged.

In order that the activist should be clear on this at first difficult issue, the matter should be summarised. Remember, the control systems of press and media are geared to make you enter the false dialectic of left and right, rulers and radicals, liberation of workers, deviants and so on. However tempting it is to attack a 'king' for his obvious and undeniable shirk in claiming kingship, it is a serious distraction which could cost you your life. It is the red cape of the matador - not the matador.

To think 'politically' is irrelevant to recognition of the power mechanisms of modern society. To think 'economically' is to accept the politico/economic divide. Using the currently indoctrinated viewpoint of media is similar to playing checkers while the opponent plays chess. Thus you hold only pawns while the enemy can deploy its forces hierarchically on the board, with a variety of sophisticated moves which you cannot understand, not having apprehended the rules of his game.

The age of the sovereign nation is finished. It is the age of structuralist interweave of supranational and varied corporate elements, above national law, elusive of the mythical 'international law' - interfacing with governments, regimes, leaderships, multinationals, conglomerates, and the banks themselves. Its hermeneutic control system is coded into the language of market values and movements. Currency value, commodity value, futures options, stock exchange method, all these play in the game of the world banking system. It controls corporate productivity and dictates what should be produced. Its most rewarding product is high technology armaments, as this ever-changing market of lethal weaponry provides the highest and quickest return. Thus it is a system dedicated - without any moral examination - to the need for a war scenario, always, somewhere, with the threat of nuclear war its strongest piece on the board to control both market and political short-term activity.

The banking entity is a pharaonic tower reaching to the heavens in its ambitious unified structure. It is a pyramid whose vast effectiveness is nevertheless based on the ordinary person's contribution to the local bank with his checking account. Any idea that you are being halal by simply rejecting interest payments must be discarded as utterly mistaken. In fact you are strengthening the enemy by giving them the money which will nevertheless accrue. The withdrawal of the poor Turkish immigrants back interest from these Berlin banks would bring about the collapse of the banks almost immediately. Yet they have been duped by a leadership which is none other than the modernist 'Islamic movement' whose role is to negotiate Islam into the banking system, something which can only be done by deliberately distorting the clear evidence of Book and Sunna. There is no clean position vis-à-vis the banking system - if you use paper money you are part of the monolithic system and are its powerful support. Only by effecting damage and causing the superstructure to collapse can the Muslim have a clean relationship with the shayatin of the monetary system and its usurious method. That is, only by taking up the Jihad declared in the Qur'an, as we noted.

JIHAD

There are many famous ayats in the Book of Allah and many renowned and authentic Hadith on the subject of Jihad.

Allah the Exalted says:

> O Believers, shall I show you a commerce that shall save you from a painful doom? You should believe in Allah and His Messenger and should fight in the way of Allah with your wealth and your lives. (61: 10-11)

> Surely Allah has bought from the believers their lives and their wealth against the gift of paradise: they fight in the way of Allah: they kill, and are killed: that is a promise binding upon Allah in the Torah and the Injil and the Qur'an, and who fulfills his contract more truly than Allah? Rejoice then in your bargain that you have made, for that is the mighty triumph. (9: 11)

> Those of the believers who hold back - unless they have an injury - are not the equals of those who fight in the way of Allah with their wealth and lives. Allah has

> granted a higher rank to those who fight with their wealth and their lives over the ones who hold back. And to each Allah has promised good, and Allah has distinguished those who strive and fight above those who sit (at home) by a special reward, ranks specially given by Him and forgiveness and mercy. For Allah is ever-forgiving, merciful (4: 95-96)

> So let those fight in the way of Allah who sell the present life for the world to come, and whoever fights in the way of Allah whether he is killed or has victory, soon shall We give him a mighty reward. (4: 74)

In the *Sahih* of Bukhari we find on the isnad of Abu Hurayra:

> A man came to the Messenger of Allah, may Allah bless him and grant him peace, and said, "Show me a task equal to Jihad." The Messenger of Allah replied, may Allah bless him and grant him peace, "There is none!"

Also in the *Sahih*: on the isnad of Anas ibn Malik:

> Truly, an early morning departure in the way of Allah or a late re-

> turn from it is better than the world and what is in it.

Also in the *Sahih* on the isnad of Abu Hurayra:

> Truly there are a hundred grades in Paradise which Allah has prepared for those who fight in a Jihad, between one grade and another is as great as between the heaven and the earth.

Also in the *Sahih* on the isnad of Zayd ibn Khalid:

> He who equips a fighter in the way of Allah or looks after a fighter's family at home is as good as one who fought.

In the *Muwatta'* of Imam Malik we find:

> Yahya related to me from Malik from Abu'z-Zinad from al-A'raj from Abu Hurayra that the Messenger of Allah, may Allah bless him and grant him peace, said, "Someone who does Jihad in the way of Allah is like someone who fasts and prays constantly and who does not slacken from his prayer and fasting until he returns." (21.1.1)

We also find:

> Yahya related to me from Malik from Abu'z-Zinad from al-A'raj from Abu Hurayra that the Messenger of Allah, may Allah bless him and grant him peace, said, "Allah guarantees either the Garden or a safe return to his home with whatever he has obtained of reward of booty, for the one who does Jihad in His way, if it is solely Jihad and trust in His promise that brings him out of his house." (21.1.2)

The psychology of the mujahid is perfectly defined in the sublime riwayat from 'Umar ibn al-Khattab in the *Muwatta'*:

> Yahya related to me from Malik from Yahya ibn Sa'id that 'Umar ibn al-Khattab said, "The nobility of the mumin is his taqwa. His deen is his noble descent. His manliness is his good character. Boldness and cowardice are but instincts which Allah places wherever He wills. The coward shrinks from defending even his father or mother, and the bold one fights for the sake of the combat not for the spoils, Being slain is but one way of meeting death, and the shahid is the one who gives himself, expectant of reward from Allah."

The need for deep personal understanding of Jihad and its motives and psychology are part of the armour of the mujahid. In the deliberately censored version of Islam which is now all but the open and official policy from every islamic organisation and Islamic Affairs Ministry, Jihad is merely a rhetorical term. Some talk of Jihad of the nafs as its real meaning without textual authority, others insist that Islam was spread by rational argument and persuasion - a quite astonishing and indeed ludicrous viewpoint. What does such a view have to do with the Ansar who were being made shahid at such a rate that it became necessary to gather and record the Qur'an in the 'Uthmani recension we now all use and acknowledge? What does that have to do with the Khalif 'Umar, may Allah be pleased with him, whose answered prayer had been: "O Allah, I ask you for martyrdom in Your way, and death in the city of Your Messenger"? No, Islam's necessary component is Jihad. Yet today the Muslim heartland is possessed by the dialectics of human greed and passion for the deen of the kuffar. The lure of jewish culture that is offered on television has captivated the Arab nation of Islam and sold us into slavery. Haram trade, which is nothing other than usury, has become the false sunna which has replaced Jihad. Thus, even the Muslim students' organisations are funded with monies invested in the usurious kafir system.

In the *Sahihayn* we discover, on the authority of 'Amr ibn 'Awf, that the Messenger, may Allah bless him and grant him peace, ordered Abu 'Ubayda ibn al-Jarrah to go and collect the Jizya from Bahrain. When Abu 'Ubayda arrived with the Jizya, the

Ansar heard of it. After praying with the Messenger, may Allah bless him and grant him peace, they surrounded him. He smiled and said, "I think you have heard that Abu 'Ubayda has brought something from Bahrain?" He then told them to be glad and hope for the good. Then he stated:

> By Allah it is not your poverty I am afraid of, rather I fear that your worldly condition be too pleasant as it had been for those before you, and you would compete for it as they did and it may destroy you as it destroyed them.

Also in the *Sahihayn* from 'Uqba ibn 'Amir we find that the Messenger of Allah, may Allah be pleased with him, prayed over the dead from the battle of Uhud. He then mounted the minbar and said:

> I am the one who goes before you and I will be a witness to you. By Allah, I am now looking on my Pond. I am given the keys of the earth and by Allah I only fear lest you compete with one another for earthly goods.

'Uqba said, 'It was the last time I saw the Messenger on the *minbar*. May Allah bless him and grant him peace.'

Today, because of the greed of the powerful in the society and because of the fantastical figures of mythical wealth - billions of so-called petro-dollars given to the leadership of the Arab community - utterly worthless paper with which they are then obliged to purchase vast arms caches to defend their raw materials - how? - which in fact are the bought property of the kuffar, delude men into believing they are wealthy and in power. The myth of development - and surely there is no more cynically untrue term than that, when all we see is increase in poverty, suffering, and kafir-enslavement - the promise of progress and limitless billions in wealth has misled the leaders and the university-indocrinated youths to believe in the fantasy power of zero-worth money. In order, therefore, to cling to some unitarian remnant of Islam they are then required to deny the obligations of Jihad, the practice of the Messenger himself, may Allah bless him and grant him peace, and the noble actions of the Salaf. Thus the modern man is afraid to fight, having lost the true orientation of the Salaf which is most clearly defined in the magnificent statement above by 'Umar ibn al-Khattab, may Allah be pleased with him.

The young Muslim reading what follows is going to be shocked again and again but he must remember that this is a Salafi Islam, nothing is invented. This was the primal pattern that led to victory - swift and Divinely promised victory. The young muslim has been taught to be 'nice' - to get on with jew and Christian - and we have seen what the unequivocal orders of Allah, glory be to Him, are on the subject. He has been told not to be fanatical, not to be an idealist dreaming of a theocratic state. All this is their language to intimidate us, make us feel inhibited - and most of all deter us from action.

Look at their actions. Look what they have done to the human race. Look at how they have humiliated and degraded women while using a rhetoric of liberation. Look how they have destroyed the stability of marriage, the sensible upbringing of children, the natural balance of sexuality, look at how every aspect of life has been 'commercialised' until there is no humanity left, nothing but delinquency, sexual deviance, lonely adults outside marriage, abandoned old people - all in the name of their progress and their development. Prisons, genocide, torture, terror - that is the rule of kuffar. Only one people can oppose them and win - the people who fight in the way of Allah under the guidance of the Messenger's noble Sunna.

One thing is certain - if the kuffar accept us and approve of us and claim they can live alongside us, then we have lost our Islam.

Annexed totally by the kuffar, it will come as a surprise to the young Muslim to find that so much of what he has accepted, not only as 'all right', but as admirable, is nothing other than the deen of the enemy. The whole body-worshipping mushrik cult of Olympic (fire-worshipping) sport is something unacceptable. The shameful rash of football clubs and adulation in the Arab nation is but one example of accepting the deen of the enemy. Anas ibn Malik reported: Allah's Messenger came to Madina. They had two festivals set aside for sports. May Allah bless him and grant him peace said, "What are these two days?" They answered, "In the time of the jahiliyya we used to practise sport during them." The Messenger, may Allah bless him and grant him peace, answered them:

> Truly, instead of these Allah has given you two better ones - the Day of Adha and the Day of Fitr.

This is from Abu Dawud:

Nor can we take retreat from the duties of the time in private illuminations and searching only for personal inner tranquillity. Abu Dawud also reports:

> A man asked the Messenger of Allah, may Allah be pleased with him, "Messenger of Allah, grant me permission for *siyahah* (roaming the land, like a darwish)." He replied to the man, "Siyahah for my community means Jihad."

So in this noble Hadith we see that even to gain spiritual inner enlightenment, Jihad is the Path. Our spirituality depends upon it.

There are others who have believed somehow without ever examining the Book of Allah that the Christians and the jews are to be tolerated as 'People of the Book'. Yet Allah declared:

> They are kafir who say Allah is the Massiah, son of Mary...

and also:

> They are kafir who say Allah is

> one of three in a trinity; for there
> is no god except God the One (5:
> 75-76)

And while the deadly enemy of Islam, the Vatican, actively plots the enslavement of the Muslims, the Pope sends 'Eid greetings to the Muslims, and it is nowhere fiercely repudiated.

Allah, glory be to Him, says:

> There are indeed many among
> the priests and monks who in
> falsehood devour the substance
> of men and hinder from the way
> of Allah. And there are those who
> bury gold and silver and spend it
> not in the way of Allah: announce
> to them a most grievous penalty.
> (9: 34)

There is no escaping the duty of the Muslims in this age.

Allah, glory be to Him, says:

> O you who believe - devour not
> usury, doubled and multiplied.
> But fear Allah that you may pros-
> per. Fear the Fire which is pre-
> pared for the kafirun. And obey
> Allah and the Messenger that you
> may obtain mercy. (3: 130-132)
>
> O you who believe - if you obey

> the kafirun they will drive you
> back on your heels, and you will
> turn back (from Islam) to your
> own loss. (3: 149)

So it is to a solemn and implacable duty that we are called. In it we are assured the victory, and in it we are assured a noble station and forgiveness from Allah. This is His promise as we have stated from His Book.

Jihad is an obligation on the people by His word, exalted is He:

> Fighting is ordained for you
> although you dislike it. But it is
> possible that you dislike a thing
> which is good for you and that
> you love a thing which is bad for
> you. But Allah knows and you
> know not. (2: 216)

Also, the Messenger of Allah, may Allah bless him and grant him peace, said, and it is reported by Abu Dawud:

> Jihad is incumbent on you with
> an Amir, whether dutiful or of
> wrong action.

Ibn Juzayy in his *Qawanin* says:

> It is a collective duty according to
> the accepted opinion.

Khalil in his *Mukhtasar* says:

> Jihad (is fought) on the side where (the enemy is) most active, (carried out) every year, even if one fears brigands, is, like the visit to the Ka'ba, a collective duty.

The obligation of Jihad remains binding upon the Muslim community after the time of the Companions, on account of the word of Allah:

> And fight them until persecution is no more and the deen is Allah's. (2: 193)

and:

> And fight them until persecution is no more and deen is all for Allah. (8: 39)

As-Suyuti says in his *Takmila* explaining 'until persecution is no more', that that means until shirk exists no more. That is also the view of Ibn 'Abbas. So it means that Jihad continues until the deen of Islam has prevailed and is dominant.

Six Conditions Make Jihad Obligatory

Ibn Juzayy says in his *Qawanin*:

They are six:

1. Islam.
2. Maturity.
3. Sanity.
4. Free birth.
5. Male sex.
6. Physical ability (bodily and financial).

Khalil in the *Mukhtasar* says:

It does not apply (Jihad) in (ten) cases:

1. Illness.
2. Childhood.
3. Madness.
4. Blindness.
5. Lameness.
6. Female sex.
7. Inability to support a dependent.
8. Slavery.
9. A debt due to be repaid.
10. When parents stop their sons (from a collective duty such as going to sea or facing danger,) though a grandfather cannot)

Six Rules of Jihad

Ibn Juzayy says in his *Qawanin:*

1. Intention.
2. Obedience to the Imam.

3. Avoidance of cheating in the ghanima (booty).
4. Respect for the pledges of protection.
5. Endurance under attack.
6. Avoidance of corruption.

Another minor mischief of the rewritten modernist, and thus toothless, Islam is that fighting is forbidden in the sacred months. This confusion is deliberate but arises from their necessary denial of abrogated and abrogating ayats. The forbidding of fighting in the sacred months is abrogated by His words:

> Fight the mushrikun altogether as they fight you altogether. (9: 36)

As-Suyuti explains this as meaning, 'on all of them and in all months.' Sa'id ibn al-Musayyab and Sulayman ibn Yasar said, and they are among the great Salaf:

> Fighting is allowed in the sacred month and the ayat is abrogated by Allah's word, 'Slay the mushrikun wherever you find them;' and by His word, 'And wage war on the mushrikun totally', that is whether in the sacred months or any other time.

Jihad is Undertaken Against Three Groups

Ibn Juzayy says in his *Qawanin*:

> There are three categories:
>
> 1. The kuffar.
> 2. Rebels.
> 3. Brigands.
>
> As to the kuffar, all types of them should be fought. But all are in agreement that women, boys, hermits and decrepit old men should not be killed unless it is feared they will be a source of danger and intrigues. The insane, the blind, and the chronically ill should not be killed unless the latter two plan intrigue.

Khalil in the *Mukhtasar* says:

> Kill them...except women, unless they engaged in the fighting, boys, the insane, the decrepit, old men, the chronically ill, the blind, and monks secluded in monasteries or hermitages provided they do not conspire, and (if not killed) only the bare minimum of provisions should be left for them.

Priests in their churches, unlike recluse worshipping monks, should, of course, be killed without any exception. Malik in the *'Utbiyya* included nuns along with monks, and said that they deserved killing even more.

It should be mentioned that evidence from Ibn Juzayy and Khalil is in every case a judgement based on a Qur'anic injunction or a Sunna and does not contain any free-floating opinions.

Ibn Juzayy says in the *Qawanin*:

> Free-born adult Muslims are first to be called. The slave with his master's permission may take part. So may strong adolescents. Unbelievers may not take part.

This is also supported by Ibn Rushd. Its source is, of course, in the Sunna. It is recorded in the *Sahih* of Muslim that when the Messenger, may Allah's blessings and peace be upon him, was marching on Badr a man known for his heroism and courage overtook him at a place called Harrat al-Wabra. The Companions were overjoyed when they saw him. The Messenger, may Allah bless him and grant him peace, asked, "What brings you here?" He replied, "I came to serve you or to take my share with you." He was then asked, "Do you believe in Allah and His Messenger?" He replied, "No." The Messenger answered, may Allah bless him and grant him peace, "Then go back. I will not take help from a mushrik." Then he came to the Messenger, may Allah bless him and grant him peace, at a place called ash-Shajar. (The same thing happened and the man was sent away.) When he came the third time, the Messenger, may Allah bless him and grant him peace, asked him, "Do you believe in Allah and His Messenger?" He said, "Yes." The Messenger, may Allah bless him and grant him peace, said, "Then join us."

Thus we have no doubts that it is an ordinance, binding, obligatory, in continuance. Jihad in the way of Allah, is not something belonging to another day, but the urgent necessity for the survival of Islam. We know well the five pillars - but the pillars are only the support of the House. Pillars without a House are nothing but a ruin. The House of Islam is complete and secure when it is adorned by Jihad in the prescribed manner, which is that war is waged on the kuffar of Dar al-Harb. Its parameters are those frontiers which delineate the kafir banking and monetary system in all its ramifications as has been demonstrated by the noble ayat. The uncompromising view of the Messenger, may Allah bless him and grant him peace, is shown in these blessed words:

> Yahya related to me from Malik from Yahy aibn Sa'id from Abu Salih as-Samman from Abu Hurayra that the Messenger of Allah, may Allah bless him and grant him peace, said, "Had I not been concerned for my community I would have liked never to stay behind a raiding party going out in the way of Allah... I would

like to fight in the way of Allah and be killed, then brought to life so I could be killed, and then brought to life so I could be killed." (*Al-Muwatta'* 21.18.40)

THE FIVE ELEMENTS OF JIHAD

We have indicated that continuous Jihad is declared by Allah and His Messenger, may Allah bless him and grant him peace, against usury. Further, we have indicated that political-national structures are no longer sovereign and effective entities, but rather that the power structures of today operate across the national grids as it were, overlapping their systems and methods by a series of interlocking webs of both commodities and currencies and the corporate stock mechanism, as well as the manipulative centres of control, the stock exchanges and options markets, in key places across the globe. Since both 'east' and 'west' participate in this world monetary system, its masters are in effect the world's masters. They are not structured in the manner the political mind has been (deliberately) trained to observe and this quite sophisticated intellect often fails to see the power mechanisms in operation. The masses see political leaders of oil countries but they are not aware of the mega-corporation president whose wealth is at issue there and who placed the leader there in the first place. (Who put the Shah in power - and who decided to move him out?)

This is not to deny the substantive physical powers that national governments do wield - but it must never be forgotten that they are the obedient servants of these non-conspiratorial, unhidden, yet unperceived power structures which represent the banking and armaments and commodities elite. What must be understood is that it is the debt system and the fantastical trillion dollar loans and interest-gathering debts which are the signifiers in the language of modern power realities. It is theoretically impossible to shift the tyranny of modern statism by revolution, since it itself was one of the jewish dialectical means to overthrow the pre-structuralist Christian rule. The monetary system is pyramidic, binary, and wide-based, so unbudgeable. Indeed, any trauma will, far from weakening the structure, strengthen it. It is only an internal attack against the total outer form, as it were, that can break the pyramid.

It is imperative therefore that war be waged both specifically and against the larger totality before victory is possible. Archive system, individual terminal, national debt - all these must be targetted. It is already well-known what the reneging of one country on its massive debt would do to the total market stability. No one has yet contemplated the impact of one destroyed Stock Exchange or Central Bank Archive.

It is by this war that the apparently unbudgeable national pseudo-entities will unlock and political power can be effectively taken over from the puppet regimes of the mega-bankers. Do not forget that Muslim 'socialist' countries accrue massive debts to the capitalist banks as well as the unfortunate countries with 'kings', as they so arrogantly style themselves.

The most serious of all undertakings cannot be made without the clearest theoretical foundations. It is imperative that Jihad is fought according to Book and Sunna. Now, Jihad has five elements. These five elements are probably either just names from the past or unknown to the young Muslim today. This is due to the revisionism of the modernist school whose role it was to enslave the Muslim masses by introducing the mythic 'Islamic banking' which would forever trap them in the jewish banking ethos.

More than this the young muslims have been conditioned to frown on these elements as primitive, aggressive, and backward. They have even been told that Islam came to abolish them - when they are its social foundations and the source of Islamic power. It is essential that the reader examine the material that follows with detachment and without intellectual panic, for the brainwashing that has already been done by the Egyptian and Pakistani modernists is very far-reaching. The evidence that follows is Islam - Book and Sunna - as understood by the fuqaha' and 'ulama' for the first thousand years of Islam. Yet, to confirm its authenticity we will take our sources from the Salaf and the Sunna-based 'ulama'. We could say that this was common knowledge until the first European infiltration of our 'ulama' that followed the French invasion of Egypt and the first subversion of Islam from within through the masonic movement. From then on this vocabulary of war on which Islamic political power was based began to disappear and be degraded, until it was viewed as undesirable and 'backward'. Of course it **WAS** undesirable to the kuffar who plotted the downfall of Islamic dominance. It must be remembered that they have succeeded. If they like our thesis - that would make it suspect. We were informed by the official national Islamic Affairs bureau of one major Islamic country that they could let us have books for new Muslims which 'would not cause offence to the modern mind' - and that we should co-operate and work with jew and Christian. It is against this background as well as the bitter fact of our age - that the massacre of Muslims whether in India, Palestine, Turkey or Syria is met with total indifference by the kuffar 'humanists' - that what follows must be reviewed.

What follows proposes the reactivation of Islamic power and effectiveness. It offers the enslaved world a way out of the intolerable debt system of haram usury - of victory for the forces of Islam - in the same morning.

THE FIVE ELEMENTS

Jihad functions on five elements: without these Jihad remains a rhetoric without a means of execution. All these are from the Book of Allah and the Sunna:

1. JIZYA.
2. DHIMMA.
3. GHAZWAT
4. 'ABEED.
5. GHANIMA.

These five we will now review in a triad of concepts - Jizya and the Dhimma first. The Ghazwat. Lastly, 'Abeed and Ghanima.

Al-Jizya wa'dh-Dhimma

As was seen above from the record of the Sunna, Jizya was collected under the Messenger of Allah, may Allah bless him and grant him peace, and the people of the Dhimma were existent and defined legally at the time of the Sahaba. It is a sign of the tragic decay of the Islamic ethos that these vital political realities have been removed not only historically but intellectually from the muslim understanding.

It is significant that the jews tried to break the law of the Dhimma, and thus Jizya, under the Mamluke governance at Damascus in 1302 of Christian dating. The law had been eroded under the corrupt Fatimid who had allowed the jews to regain their sinister ascendency again. Encouraged, they made a claim under a document purporting to date back to the time of the Messenger, may Allah bless him and grant him peace. The Qadi before whom the appeal came was none other than Ibn Taymiyya, who proved the document a fake, re-instituted the Jizya and also forced the jews to pay back-taxes from the time they had lapsed in payment.

The Dhimma is a social contract of protection between the Muslims and the kuffar. By it they are taxed and that tax is in lieu of the Zakat which they do not pay, and it secures from the Muslims protection and safety. The Jizya is that tax paid by the dhimmi.

Here is one section of the contract of the Ahl adh-Dhimma made by the Khalif 'Umar ibn al-Khattab, may Allah be pleased with him:

> We shall respect the Muslims, stand up for them in our assemblies should they choose to sit in them. We shall not imitate them in any of our garments - whether caps or turbans, sandals or in parting the hair. We shall not imitate them in their speech. We shall not adopt their surnames. We shall not purchase or carry weapons. Our mounts will not be saddled. We will not wear swords. We will not wear signet rings inscribed in Arabic. We will not sell wine. We will clip the

> forepart of our hair, wear our own style of clothing, and wear belts. We shall not expose the cross over our churches nor make public display of the cross. Our religious books will not be displayed in street or market frequented by Muslims. Bells will only be allowed to ring softly within the churches. We shall not raise our voices at funerals, nor light fires in procession along Muslim streets.

How would 'Umar ibn al-Khattab in the light of that document, view the relationship of, say, the technocratic elite of the petro-chemical industries, who are kuffar, with the immigrant workers from Pakistan, who are Muslim, in the Gulf and on the Arabian peninsula? How do we view it?

Here is the Khalif 'Umar on the same subject again:

> Do not exchange correspondence with dhimmis in case friendship should grow between you and them. Do not call them by their formal names. They must be kept in their place but not wronged. Command their women not to tighten their waistbands, and not to let their forelocks hang over their faces. Also they should be made to stand in the marketplace so that they can be distin-

> guished from muslim women. If they refuse, they had better embrace Islam - willingly or unwillingly.

The great Islamic leader, 'Umar ibn 'Abd al-'Aziz met with a group of the Bani Taghlib. They were wearing turbans like Muslims. "O, Amir al-Mumineen, count us as among the Muslims." To this he asked, "Who are you?" They replied, "We are Christians." "Get me some scissors!" commanded the Amir. He cut off their forelocks, tore off their turbans, then cut a strip from the bottom of their cloaks and gave them to them as waistbands. He then ordered, "You must not use saddles. Only pack-saddles. And you must let your legs down on one side of your horses."

Further, 'Umar ibn 'Abd Al-'Aziz issued an order to this effect:

> Stop the christians from wearing cloaks, silks and turbans. Enforce this order. Publicise it. The order must not be ignored by anyone. It has been reported to me that lots of Christians under your authority have stopped wearing the *zunnar* (belt), constantly use turbans while letting their hair hang over their ears and shoulders. If this has been done inside the domain of your authority it is a sign of your weakness and failure. See to it that my commands are now

carried out without either leniency or concession.

The restrictions which were carried out in the time of the Abbasid Khalif, al-Mutawakkil, were done in consultation with Imam Ahmad ibn Hanbal. Thus one can see a continuity of both practice and viewpoint from the time of the Salaf on to the later chanting, bell-ringing, torchlight processions. All these things were forbidden under the Dhimma. The Ahl adh-Dhimma were looked down on and respect was denied them. Today it is the Muslim who is despised as his so-called leaders in Islamic learning rush to attend Conferences in Rome, mingling with Bishops, kissing their rings, sending us their 'Eid cards in place of the Christmas cards they would so dearly like to send. As if that were not enough, they sit together with the rabbis under the shadow of the jewish candlesticks, reading out from the Torah while the rabbis ask to have our 'brotherhood' with them confirmed by permission to visit Makka and Madina. This happened in London.

Either it is they who are under our orders or it is we who are their bought slaves. The issues are so clear and until there is this psychological view of the kuffar and until it is seen that there is a mechanism to reassert our vigour and power, we will remain under their dominance; that is, if we do not find ourselves the victims of their genocidal fury yet again.

Indeed, the distinction between the dhimmis and the Muslims which was the cornerstone of 'Umar's power as Khalif found its deepest political significance in the Islamic rejection of kafir languages and in the spiritual and linguistic superiority of Arabic over other tongues. The order of 'Umar on the subject was:

> Do not learn the blethering (*ratana*) of the 'ajamis, nor visit the mushrikun in their churches on their holidays, for Allah's anger descends on them.

How interesting a motto for the hordes of Arab students who leave the Muslim heartland every year for Europe and America, innocent and eager, ready to 'get the know-how' and yet somehow maintain their Islam. Of course, they get the know-how - they know how to be good modern kuffar - for that is precisely what a western education is. "After studying anthropology," declared an American university text book on the subject, "do not worry that you will not necessarily go on to become an anthropologist; what matters to us is that you have learned to think like us."

Let us now examine the direct application of the matter concerning the dhimmis and the Jizya, Theoretically, it is obligatory to invite the kuffar to Islam before fighting them.

In the *Sahih* of Bukhari we find:

> The Messenger of Allah, may Allah bless him and grant him peace, gave the standard to 'Ali on the day of Khaybar, who

asked him, "O Messenger of Allah, shall I fight them until they become (Muslims) like ourselves?" The Messenger, may Allah bless him and grant him peace, replied, "Go out at your leisure until you reach their place. Then invite them to Islam and tell them what their duty is towards Allah, for, by Allah, that He should guide a single man through you is better than owning the choicest camels of the herd."

In the *Mukhtasar* of Khalil it says:

> Invite them to Islam: then Jizya (that is, if they do not accept).

In the *Qawanin* of Ibn Juzayy it says:

> Invitation to Islam before fighting is only for those whom the call to Islam has not previously reached. They should be invited to it first. If they accept they are to be spared. If they refuse, the alternative of Jizya is to be offered. If they refuse this, then they are to be fought. But as regards those to whom the call to Islam has already come, they should not be called again and the most unex-

pected time should be sought (to attack).

Since the modern kuffar are all too aware what Islam means, some, it would appear, better than the young Muslims, it may be that one could proceed without the call. If it is to be made, and correctness is essential, it should be made generally, and not in a way which will tactically strengthen the enemy against you.

It is important to realise, however, the realistic conditions for collecting Jizya.

In the *Mukhtasar* Khalil says:

> They are to be summoned to Islam, then (if they refuse, they must pay the) Jizya, (if the Muslims are) in a place safe from their intrigues.

In other words, they can only be summoned when the place is secure under the Muslims' hands; equally, one can only collect Jizya when there is a domain under our fuqaha'. If, however, they could attack us they should be fought without delay - without, that is, the call or the alternative of the tax.

Al-jizyat al-'anwiyya is Jizya under compulsion within the process of Jihad.
Al-jizyat as-sulhiyya is Jizya by agreement within the Dar al-Islam.

In the light of the condition of the Muslims in this age it is clear that, at least in the first phase of the Jihad, we cannot run the risk of the summons and the Jizya - although the summons can be made generally and publically without revealing the first targets of the Jihad and its striking force.

Ibn Abi Zayd al-Qayrawani says in his *Risala*:

> The Jizya tax is due on the people of the dhimma, that is, the free adult males but not their wives, nor children pre-puberty, nor their slaves. It is equally due on fire-worshippers and Christian Arabs. For those who use gold the tax is four dinars. For those who use silver it is forty dirhams. The tax is reduced for the poor. Take from the dhimmis who do business from country to country one tenth of the price of what they sell, and this on each journey abroad. If they import to Makka or Madina then the tax is only one twentieth. For the businessmen under the category of Dar al-Harb, the tax is one tenth on entering the Muslim land, unless they submit to a higher tax.

From all this it can be seen that the Jizya is a tax most likely to be significant after the first stage of the new Jihad. However, the psychological and political view of the kuffar entailed in the concept of ahl adh-dhimma is essential to the Salafi's Islam, and a powerful part of a world-view based on the Book and the Sunna. Also, the low view of the dhimmi is something of urgent importance to the Muslim today while surrounded by an ignorant and arrogant world of kuffar who think themselves superior to Muslims while displaying the most decadent and disgusting anti-human behaviour. Not taking the jews and Christians as friends, not following their deen, not submitting to bid'a, neither in holidays (National Days, etc.) nor in habits, not entering their places of worship, nor participating in their festivals - all this is vital in the prelude to the attack of the new Jihad.

Khalil says in the *Mukhtasar* speaking of both sulhi and 'anwi dhimmis:

> The dhimmi is forbidden the horse, the mule, the saddle, the main roads. He must wear a distinguishing dress, and be punished for not wearing the *zunnar* (belt). He is (punished) for drunkenness in public places, for making his religious views manifest, for careless talk (about Muslims). Wine is to be poured away (if produced in public), and the church bells destroyed.

> The dhimmi has repudiated his agreement if he act thus:

1. Fights (against Muslims).
2. Withholds payment of Jizya.
3. Rebels against (Muslim) legal decisions.
4. Rapes a freeborn Muslim woman.
5. Pretends to her (that he is Muslim to marry her).
6. Informs (the enemy) about the weak points in the Muslim defences.
7. Insults a Prophet with slander over and above what constitutes his unbelief.

(In these cases) he should be put to death unless he professes Islam. (Obligatory on 4, 5 and 7, the others are discretionary.) If a dhimmi leaves Dar al-Islam and is caught he is to be enslaved, provided no injustice has been done to him. But if it is for an injustice he is not to be enslaved.

Ibn Juzayy in his *Qawanin* lists the obligations of the dhimmi:

1. They must pay the Jizya outright in a state of abasement.
2. They must entertain passing Muslims as guests for three days.
3. Pay one tenth on the trade they carry out beyond the area in which they live.

4. They should not build a church; nor leave one standing in an area built up by the Muslims, if it is Muslim by force. If dhimmi by sulh the church may remain if already there.
5. They may not ride fine horses or mules but only donkeys.
6. They may not use the main roads but stick to the narrow ones.
7. They must wear distinguishing clothing such as the belt.
8. They must not cheat the Muslims nor shelter a spy.
9. They should not hinder the Muslims from putting up at their churches day or night.
10. They should respect the Muslims. They should not beat a Muslim nor abuse him nor take him into service.
11. Gongs and bells should be hidden. No religious rites should be public.
12. They should not slander any Prophet nor display their religious convictions openly.

Our obligations to them are:

1. We may let them settle in any land except the Arabian

peninsula, that is, the Hijaz and the Yemen.
2. We should leave them in peace: guarantee protection to them and their property.
3. We should not interfere with their churches, nor with their wine or pigs unless they make them public. If they show their wine publically we should throw it at them. If one of them brings out a pig in public he is to be punished.

How is it possible to read the nominative rules of Islam and not reflect on how the Muslims of Palestine came to lose their freedom - at the hands of those who took from them their means of power, modernist 'ulama', who tried to be pleasing to the enemy, and denied these sunan.

Ghazwat

The Jihad is under specific rules and parameters and phases. We have noted the preliminary phases that may, under certain circumstances be practised. We have also observed how - even if not practised - they remain built into the process psychologically, both in the awareness of the end purpose of the Jihad, to bring the kuffar into Islam and make the Deen altogether Allah's, and in the need to be aware of the despicable nature of the enemy.

Then the Jihad itself consists of specific actions, encounters, raids - which make up the over-all strategy of the war itself, something which theoretically does not end until the Last Day.

Thus the Jihad moves immediately into the operational phase. The first raiding parties are often seen as raising the means for the Jihad itself - this by the acquisition of wealth and personnel by booty and slavery - the sciences of which we will shortly examine, *insha'llah*. What is important here is to recognise how the view of the ghazwat should fit the age we live in and the enemy against whom we are at war - the banking entity and its world-wide tentacles.

Ghazwat - raiding parties - are a noble and blessed sunna. We have already mentioned how exalted they were in the eyes of the Messenger, may Allah bless him and grant him peace. We saw that he would have liked nothing better than to die in the fight, be raised up, die again, be raised only to be slain a third time.

In the *Muwatta'* we find:

> Yahya related to me from Malik that he had heard that 'Umar ibn 'Abd al-'Aziz wrote to one of his governors, "It has been passed down to us that when the Messenger of Allah, may Allah bless him and grant him peace, sent out a raiding party, he would say to them, 'Make your raids in the

name of Allah in the way of Allah. Fight whoever denies Allah. Do not steal from the booty, and do not act treacherously. Do not mutilate. And do not kill children.' Say the same to your armies and raiding parties, Allah willing. Peace be upon you." (21.3.11)

It is vital that while the attacks be of the utmost ruthlessness and effectiveness, the Islamic magnificence of the raiders be maintained. The component of the fighters, as we shall later see, *insha'llah*, must contain both annihilation and pardon, following the command of Allah, glory be to Him, and the practice of His Messenger, may Allah bless him and grant him peace.

> Yahya related to me from Malik from Humayd at-Tawil from Anas ibn Malik that when the Messenger of Allah, may Allah bless him and grant him peace, went out to Khaybar, he arrived at night, and when he came upon a people by night, he did not attack until morning. In the morning the jews came out with their spades and baskets. When they saw him they said, "Muhammad! By Allah! Muhammad and his army!" The Messenger of Allah, may Allah bless him and grant him peace, said, "Allahu akbar! Khaybar is destroyed. When we come to a

> people, it is an evil morning for
> those who have been warned."
> (21.19.48)

It should be remembered that in the early phase of the Jihad, raiding should be on the targets of all who participate in the haram usurious practice, and that the jews have enhanced their power, that is, the worthless paper money, by their own hoards of wealth, through control of the diamond and the gold markets, and that these centres of hoarded wealth are among the necessary first targets to finance the larger struggle.

We see from the above Hadith that the Sunna was to strike at the time least expected. It follows that one should also strike at the place not expected. By extension, in the light of the current situation, one may strike at several centres all at the same time, thus causing havoc in the enemy and in their response.

Of course, there are many famous treatises on war and its classical strategies. In order that we acquire a true Islamic perspective in our view of Jihad we take our direct inspiration and also judgement from the Qur'an, always checking most carefully that one is dealing with the abrogating and not the abrogated ayats.

Allah, glory be to Him, says:

> Make ready for them all you can
> of force and of horses tethered, to
> strike terror into the enemies of

> Allah and your enemies, and others besides whom you may not know, but whom Allah knows. Whatever you spend in the way of Allah will be repaid to you, and you will not be treated unjustly. (8: 60)

"All you can of force" - this is taken to be a permission to use any means to vanquish the enemy.

The key to Islamic warfare lies in the glorious ayat:

> O you who believe, when you meet a force, stand firm and call on Allah a lot that you may succeed. And obey Allah and His Messenger, and do not fall into disputes in case you lose heart and your power leaves; and be patient and persistent, for Allah is with those who patiently persevere. (8: 45-46)

The mujahid should give sadaqa, fast, or put right an injustice he has done before an operation, make salat with depth and sincerity, give counsel recommending good and warning against evil. These were the habits of 'Umar ibn al-Khattab who used to say to his soldier, "Indeed, you only fight with your actions!"

In the *Qawanin* Ibn Juzayy says:

> There is no objection to destroying their villages and forts, flooding or cutting off their water supply, or devastating the area.

In the *Mukhtasar* of Khalil we find:

> By cutting water, using any weapon or by fire if there is no other way.

Ibn Zarqun of Seville said there is agreement on fighting them with fire even though other methods are open to the fighters. He added, "If we do not throw fire at them, they will throw fire at us." This view is disputed because of the Islamic reluctance to destroy life by fire. The Messenger of Allah, may Allah bless him and grant him peace, repeated three times, "There is force in the arrows!" By this he indicated his taste for target-oriented warfare over indiscriminate destruction. However, in these matters judgement must be made in each situation, always seeking the way of most ferocious effectiveness while paying attention to the Islamic duty for the protection of women and children who are non-combatant. In such circumstances as require difficult decisions, the Muslims choose the lesser evil of two modes of destruction but remain implacable in the battle against the enemy.

In the *Mukhtasar*, Khalil says:

> If they shield themselves with children they must be left alone on account of fear, and if they

> shield themselves with a Muslim, the Muslim should not be aimed at unless there is fear for the majority of the Muslims.

It is commonly accepted that such a ruse of the enemy as the human shield demands in the end that they must be fought.

In the *Risala* of Ibn Abi Zayd al-Qayrawani:

> Running away from the enemy is a grave wrong action if the enemy are double the number of the Muslims or less: if they are more than double the number of the Muslims there is no objection to fleeing.

Ibn Juzayy in his *Qawanin* says:

> It is not allowed to desert the line of battle if that may cause defeat for the Muslims: if not, it is allowed to one manoeuvering in battle or turning aside to join another company. To manoeuvre for battle is to pretend to retreat while intending to return as a stratagem of war. Turning aside to join a company of Muslims present in the battle is allowed. Turning aside to join a company which is absent, or in a town, is a matter of dispute.

> It is not allowed to abandon battle unless the kuffar are more than double the number of Muslims. If the Muslims realise that they are certainly going to be killed then it is better for them to quit. If, furthermore, it is realised that they will be of no effect in demoralising the enemy, flight is obligatory.

Khalil says in the *Mukhtasar*:

> To flee (is forbidden) if the number of Muslims is half (of the kuffar or more) and their total strength is not up to twelve thousand, unless they are manoeuvering or turning aside to join another company if there is fear.

The next element of war to be considered involves the two remaining elements in the Islamic Jihad. As these have been made a matter of controversy and even denial by the kuffar (on our behalf) and by the collaborator-modernists, it must first be established by us that these two elements of war are both noble sunnas and authorised by Divine Decree in His Book, glory be to Him. Indeed, it is these two elements which will release the Muslims from their present bonded slavery and sense of impotence before the so-called super-powers, themselves so morally and spiritually weak. Power belongs to Allah and it is His gift to the muminun in order that they have the promised victory, fighting in the way of Allah.

It is now time to consider booty and slaves - the two incomes and rewards of the ghazwat and the Jihad and the wealth of the mujahideen and the foundation of the ensuing Islamic state.

Al-Ghanima wa'l-'Abeed

Before proceeding it is important to establish and remind the reader of that established foundation on which the Deen is built and which requires obedience from us. There is absolutely no way to a revisionist position in Islam in the sense of altering what the Messenger, may Allah bless him and grant him peace, brought, any more than one can alter what the Almighty has decreed in His Book. There is no way to suggest that now we are more enlightened, more advanced, or more modern, whatever that may mean, other than later in time and thus further in darkness. The Sunna is the light and miracle of prophethood and the necessary other component of Islam along with the Book of Allah.

Allah the Exalted says:

> Believe in Allah and the Messenger and the light which He sent down (64: 8)

> We sent you as a witness and a bringer of good news and a warn-

er so that they might believe in Allah and His Messenger (48: 8-9)

Whoever does not believe in Allah and His Messenger, We have prepared a blaze for the kafirun (48: 13)

Whoever has obeyed the Messenger has obeyed Allah. (4: 79)

Take what the Messenger brings you and leave what he forbids you. (59: 8)

In the matter of the Sunna we find further that in the Book of Allah this primacy of the Sunna demands obedience and following.

Say, if you love Allah follow me and He will love you and forgive you your wrong actions. (3: 31)

Believe in Allah and His Messenger, the unlettered prophet who believes in Allah and His words. Follow him, perhaps you will be guided. (7: 157)

The commentators say of the words in the Fatiha: "the path of those whom You have blessed" means the path of those who follow the Sunna.

There is no ambiguity among the Salaf in their position regarding the Sunna nor is there any doubt about their dedicated pursuance of it.

One of the family of Khalid ibn Asid asked 'Abdullah ibn 'Umar, 'Abu 'Abdu'r-Rahman! We find the fear prayer and the resident prayer in the Qur'an and we do not find the travelling prayer." Ibn 'Umar, may Allah be pleased with him, said, "My nephew, Allah sent Muhammad, may Allah bless him and grant him peace, and we did not know anything. We do as we saw him doing."

'Umar ibn al-Khattab, may Allah be pleased with him, wrote to his governors to learn the Sunna. He said, "People will seek to argue with you," that is, by the Qur'an, "so overcome them by the Sunna. The people of the Sunna have the most knowledge of the Book of Allah."

Ibn 'Umar said, "The travelling prayer is two rak'ats. Whoever opposes the Sunna is a kafir."

It is also the clear position that to alter any part of his command is to be in dangerous opposition, misguidance and innovation.

Allah the Exalted says:

> Whoever splits from the Messenger after the guidance is clear to him and follows other than the path of the believers, We shall entrust him to what he has turned to. (4: 114)

Now, taking the booty and sharing it, and the Messenger's, may Allah bless him and grant him peace, taking one fifth, is known and acknowledged. This was also the Sunna followed by the Salaf, and this was the habit of the Muslim armies at all times and in all places where Islam flourished in its original form of adherence to Book and Sunna, before the innovations of the modernist innovators and apologists to the western 'humanist' tradition and perfect justice for all, which was a view which included the so-called liberation of women, the exaltation of low people to high office, and the abolition of slavery.

Bound inexorably with the ghanima laws is the principle of Islamic legal slavery. Slavery in Islam is embedded in the Book of Allah and in the Sunna of the Messenger, may Allah bless him and grant him peace. Nowhere ever was there any evidence to justify that it had been abolished or altered as a fundamental part of existence. Indeed, it is part of the ordained nature of things as expressed openly in the Book.

Qadi 'Iyad, the renowned muhaddith, said in his *Ash-Shifa'*:

> We are absolutely certain about declaring a person to be a kafir who belies or denies any of the foundations of the shari'at or anything that is known by certainty to have been a deed of the Messenger, may Allah bless him and grant him peace, through transmission, or regarding which

> there has been unbroken consensus.

There are many ayats which speak at length and explicitly about slavery. One can mention specific texts such as:

> Allah has struck a metaphor: a slave who is owned and capable of nothing...

And His saying:

> ...from that which you possess by your right hands.

Indeed, the taking of slaves in the war is specifically referred to in the ayat:

> And we prescribed for them in it: a self for a self.

In all these many references in the Qur'an, while freeing a slave is seen as an act of generosity and also a giving up from one's wealth, it is absolutely nowhere suggested that this would ever imply the abolition of slavery. The view of slavery is that it is part of the human condition, and what is at issue is that it be practised with compassion and with regard to the Sunna in right treatment and in dealing with the slaves and their rights in marriage and so on.

> Do you have among those whom your right hands possess partners

> in the provision we have granted you, such that you are equals in it, you fearing them like you fear yourselves?

In the *Sahih* of Bukhari we find:

> They are your brothers. Allah has put them (slaves) under (the power of) your hands. Feed them from what you eat. Clothe them from what you wear. Do not charge them to do jobs beyond their capacity.

In the *Muwatta'* we find:

> Malik related to me that he had heard that 'Abdullah ibn 'Umar was asked whether a slave could be bought on the specific condition that it was to be used to fulfill the obligation of freeing a slave, and he said, "No." (Malik added, "There is no harm, however, in someone buying a person expressly to set him free.")

It is clear from this the that freeing of slaves takes its place along with sadaqa as a means of disciplining the self, making up for faults, and acquiring good character. It in no way indicated the cessation or the negation of the institution of slavery as part of the human contract.

Now the rhetoric and position of the kuffar on the issue of slavery, loaded as it is with emotional and theatrical appeals to humanity and justice, is one of a set of values which this monstrously inhuman society uses to control the thinking and reason of its members while all the time claiming justice and reasonability.

It must be clear to the Muslim that the so-called abolitionist position is a highly political stance. It should be recalled that the same men who were purportedly fighting for the freeing of all slaves were at the same time planning and executing the colonial policy which led to the complete disintegration of the noble Islamic civilisation of West Africa and northern Nigeria. Abolitionism was the arm of a militant christianity which saw that slavery - and remember the kafir slaving is not in any way comparable to the slavery of the Muslims who are under the strict injunctions of the shari'at - on an individual level was anachronistic when the industrial society opened the way to a much more extensive and all-controlling form of slavery, that of the technological society, that is, the concentration camp, the gulag, and indeed, the work nexus of the machine society.

In short, slavery was the humanism and they saw it as outmoded by the slave-society that was modern industrialism. The French government, founded as it is on the legends of 'liberty, fraternity and equality', dedicatedly anti-slave, can boast of the largest slave encampment in all Africa. The whole Tuareg nation is enslaved without rights of passage, without permission to travel the shortest distance.

All of northern Mali is a slave camp, so too is Niger. And lest any think that the mythic vocabulary of black/white conflict is at the heart of the slave question, they should take note that the slavers in West Africa are the black population who now work as the slave guards for the French shayatin.

As one Mauritanian 'alim put it, "We had slavery on a small scale, and under the humane conditions of Islamic law. You have made the whole world slaves." Indeed, what would you call the condition of the Palestinians in their camps, without passports or rights or country? What would you call the mass of immigrant workers on the mainland of Europe - without franchise or rights, living slaves to the industrial nexus, trapped in the menial tasks of sewage disposal and street cleaning? What would you call the condition of the Philippine and other oriental workers in the petro-chemical complexes and cities on the Arabian peninsula - do they have rights, movement, choice? No. The truth is that when slavery under Islamic law was removed, then the only just means of slavery in existence was removed and left to mankind the only alternative which is slavery without laws or limits, kafir and cruel. The gulags and the slave camps of Central America and West Africa - to say nothing of the nation of South Africa - are the slavery of the kuffar - only they do not call it slavery.

One could truly say that since the Muslims lost their slaves they lost their power and now they are all slaves of the kafir forces. It is precisely the power system of that slavery which the Jihad against the monetary system and its institutions and documentation and computerised archive is dedicated to overthrow. The road to the victory against the kafir system is one on which the return to halal slavery is a factor. For one of the immediate results of the ghazwat will be the ghanima, and with it the taking of slaves, male and female.

The United States of America has based itself on two elements. The abolition of kafir slavery and the creation of paper money *ex nihilo*, in order to float credit and increase usury beyond calculable limits. Both these factors were outside the laws of the creation as laid down by the Creator, glory be to Him. But it is the replacement of unjust slavery with lawful and limited slavery under the shari'at, and it is the foundation of just trade without usury - it is these two elements which are the necessary conditions of the post-kafir society and which we can set up wherever and whenever we commence our Jihad against usury.

We must now turn our attention to the responsibilities in the ghanima and the 'abeed which will arise following the ghazwat.

****

Ibn Juzayy says in his *Qawanin*:

>They are seven:
>
>>1. Kafir men.
>>2. Their women.
>>3. Their children.

4. Their wealth.
5. Their land.
6. Their food.
7. Their drink.

As to the men, the Imam must make a choice between five things:

1. To kill them.
2. To set them free (by generosity).
3. To set them free (by ransom)
4. Force them to pay Jizya.
5. Enslave them.

Wealth is in four categories:

1. What is entirely for Allah, which is Jizya, Kharaj (land-tax), the dhimmi's tenth-tax and people with whom peace has been contracted and any property acquired without fighting. All this is *fay'* (revenue), so the Imam may dispose of it as he sees fit. It is not divided into five.

2. That which goes to whoever has seized it, without giving up the one-fifth (*khums*). It comprises what he seizes anywhere in the land of war without going after it (*ijaf*), such as what a fleeing captive runs

away with from the kuffar and what the enemy have abandoned for fear of being drowned, except if it is gold, in which case it is treated as *rikaz* (buried treasure).

3. Booty (*ghanam*) whose fifth goes to Allah and the rest goes to whoever has seized it. This is the ghanima and the rikaz. We mean by ghanima what a man has seized by force, and in the same way, what is seized by way of stealth and strategy.

4. What there is dispute about as to whether to submit the khums or not. It comprises what slaves have seized with no free-born man accompanying them, or what is seized by women and boys with no man accompanying them or what its people leave behind without being over-run by an army.

Land falls into three classes:

1. A land far from our domination. In which case it must be razed by devastation or fire.

2. A land under our domination but not inhabited. The Imam

may hand it over to someone but the army has no right to it.

3. A nearby and desirable land. The accepted opinion is that it should be made a waqf, the kharaj of which is to be used for the welfare of the muslims to help pay for the soldiers, the officials, to construct bridges, build mosques, town walls and so on.

As for their food and drinks, they can be utilised without being divided up as long as they are in Dar al-Harb. If a large quantity remains on reaching Dar al-Islam and after the dispersal of the army one has to give it out as sadaqa. If only a little remains one can use it oneself.

On the division of the ghanima, Ibn Juzayy says in the *Qawanin*:

> The Amir calls the army roll-call. He then divides four-fifths of the ghanima among them while they are in Dar al-Harb.

On entitlement he says:

> By being present at the battle even when the booty is seized after the person has left, accord-

> ing to the generally accepted opinion...but he who falls behind on the road and abandons the campaign has no share; after entering enemy territory then his share is secure. If the army splits into two sections and each section seizes booty separately they should share out the total if each is near enough to the other to help in time of need. If a raiding party goes out from the army and captures booty in a place near enough for help from the army to reach it, the army should have a share in its booty. But if the place is far, the army should not have a share, and if the army seizes any booty after the party has gone out, the party's share is secure if they have the leader's permission to go.

The enforcement of the law in the matter of booty is vital to the moral comportment of the army and raiders. It is the grave responsibility of the army and raid-leaders. The mujahideen must be taught their Islamic duty and the Islamic viewpoint in these matters. The ghanima is certainly their due, but greed in it is reprehensible, and cheating a most serious thing.

Ibn Juzayy says in the *Qawanin*:

> Ghulul is forbidden according to 'ijma. If a man who has cheated repents before the ghanima is divided he should not be punished, and what he has taken has to be added to the spoils. If his repentance comes after the dispersal of the army, he is to be punished and his share given away as sadaqa.

Khalil in the *Mukhtasar* says:

> And ghulul, anyone found guilty of it, is to be punished.

Ghulul is defined as taking away from the booty anything which one is not allowed to, before it is duly divided.

Allah the Exalted says:

> And know that out of all the ghanima that you may acquire, a fifth share is assigned to Allah, and to the Messenger, and to near relatives, orphans, the needy and the wayfarer. (8: 41)

In the *Mukhtasar* Khalil says:

> A Muslim has to give up a fifth - even if he is a slave, according to the more correct opinion, but not if he is a dhimmi. (This last

because the ayat above addressed the muminun only.)

Ibn Juzayy in the *Qawanin* says:

> The practice of just Imams concerning fay' and khums is to begin by securing the dangerous places and frontier posts, by preparing armaments and by paying soldiers. If there remains anything it goes to the judges, state officials, and the building of mosques and bridges, and then it is divided among the poor. If any still remains the Imam has the option of either giving it to the rich or keeping it to deal with disasters which may occur to Islam.

Khalil says in the *Mukhtsar*:

> An enemy slave who embraces Islam is free if he flees to us or stays on till he is captured as booty, but not if he goes out after his master has become a Muslim.

Allah the Exalted says:

> Also (prohibited are) women already married, except those whom your right hands possess. (4: 24)

That means female captives who have been captured while still having husbands in Dar al-Harb. It is lawful to their owner to have sexual intercourse with them after waiting for the passing of one period of menstruation, because captivity nullifies the contract of marriage between her and her husband. The Messenger of Allah, may Allah bless him and grant him peace, sent an army to Awtas where they captured some women who had kafir husbands. They abstained from having sexual relations with these women so Allah revealed the above ayat. Note, the woman does not observe an 'idda since she has thus become a slave.

The *Risala* of Ibn Abi Zayd al-Qayrawani states:

> The waiting period *(istibra')* of a slave girl is the passing of one menstruation whether ownership of her changes through sale, gift, captivity or other means.

The subjects of ghanima and 'abeed are vast in detail. There are over three books of the *Muwatta'* delineating the rules of slave dealing and slave rights. What is here is enough to indicate their crucial nature in the matter of an activated Islam which intends to fulfill its historical mission by achieving victory, and by ruling, thus imposing on man the justice and the balance he so tragically lacks under kafir tyranny. Islam can only be understood as a rule of law and never as something ruled by the arbitrary principles of men, some good, some bad. It is for this reason that all forms of Constitution are a bid'a and a deliberate demotion of the Book and the Sunna as ultimate authority in the matter of the human condition.

JIHAD: FURTHER PRINCIPLES

Jihad is made against three groups:

1. Al-Kuffar.
2. Al-Bughat.
3. Al-Muharibun.

That is, the kuffar and the mushrikun, the rebels among the Muslims, and brigands.

The kuffar are in three categories:

1. The born kafir, who is jew, Christian, Magian or pagan from inheritance.
2. The Muslim who has gone out of Islam by declaration.
3. The alleged Muslim we find to be guilty of kufr by committing outward actions unacceptable to a Muslim.

The children and wives of the kuffar are made prisoner and their property divided. Of the ex-Muslims, Ibn Rushd confirmed the ruling of Ibn al-Qasim, that the children and wives should not be made captive, but their property was *fay'*. Of the third category, their children are not enslaved but they are compelled to accept Islam.

Khalil says in the *Mukhtasar*:

> If a group of people go out of Islam and wage war, they are like

those who go out.

This means the aged are called to repent and the young forced to adopt Islam. Their property is held but the children are not made captive. This is what 'Umar did, and what most scholars and the Imams agreed on. (Of course, Abu Bakr killed the men and took captive the dependents.) That 'Umar rescinded the sentence of Abu Bakr is a famous example of the suppleness and generosity of Islamic law and not a logical contradiction.

Ibn Juzayy says in the *Qawanin:*

> **Al-Baghy** - rebellion. Rebels are those who are to be fought for false interpretation, the mistaken sects like the Khawarij and others, those who revolt against the Imam or refuse to come under his sway, or withhold a lawful due such as zakat and the like. The rebels are first to be called back to the truth. If they respond, that is to be accepted from them and they are to be duly spared; if they refuse they are to be fought and it is permissible to shed their blood.
>
> **Al-Muharibun** - they must first be admonished. Then they must be warned three times in the name of Allah. If they give up (it is all right); but if not they should be fought and it is Jihad. If a brig-

and is killed no retaliation may be taken. Anyone killed by a brigand is a martyr. If a brigand is caught before he repents, the prescribed penalty should be inflicted on him, which is killing or crucifixion, or amputation of the hand or leg, or banishment. As for killing and crucifixion, they are inflicted together, the latter first according to Ibn al-Qasim. Amputation is of left leg and right hand. Banish-ment is for the free and not the slave.

It is the delight of the kuffar to read these matters and scream out that we are primitive, bloodthirsty and so on, and the weakened, western-educated or mistaught graduate of their system squirms with discomfort and disowns the laws of Islam. He then turns round to see his own brother Muslims killed by phosphorus bombs and anti-personnel bombs specifically designed to be picked up by playing children in order to maim them. He sees whole camps of Palestinian refugees genocidally destroyed by the agents of those same jews who perpetually whine about the alleged massacre of their people for the crime of usury in Europe in the thirties. They see all this and they can make no moral judgment because they have passed the means of moral discrimination from their hands to the jews and the Christians, who maintain their inquisitorial position vis-à-vis the Muslims from Indonesia to the Maghrib.

Judgments must be carried out without effeminate sentiment or weakness, and yet the orders of the Almighty must effect the heart and the intellect of the Amir.

Allah the Exalted has said:

> Those who spend, in prosperity or in adversity, who restrain anger, and pardon men - for Allah loves those who do good. (3: 134)

> The recompense for an injury is an injury equal to it, but if a person forgives and makes reconciliation his reward is due from Allah, for (Allah) loves not those who do wrong. (42: 40)

Mu'awiya, may Allah be pleased with him, said:

> I do not seek the aid of my sword, in a case where my whip would be adequate, nor my whip when my tongue would do.

Khalil comments in the *Mukhtasar:*

> For disobeying Allah or (wronging) a human being the Imam punishes by imprisonment, warning, or by making him stand up, or by removing the turban, or by beating with a whip or the like, even though he might exceed the limit (prescribed) or cause death.

The implication here is that in the case of death due to punishment no blame devolves on the Imam.

From all this it is clear that there can be no rule and no governance without fiqh. Without the fuqaha' remaining the Amir's necessary elite, uncorrupted, unafraid, able to speak out, holding to zuhd and non-involvement with the family and the wealth of the Amir, there can be no Islamic governance.

Anyone calling for the dismantling of the method of arriving at legal judgments is calling for the castration, politically speaking, of the Muslim community. Devoid of fiqh, which demands its chosen method or madh-hab, there remains only prayer-based Islam without capacity to rule on the matters confronting the current society. In that situation, the very means utilised by the Salaf are removed from the Muslims. The result is powerlessness.

An active, or let us say an activated, fiqh by one who has adopted the militant and imposing power of Islamic duties, must lead very soon to implementation of the shari'at. There can be no question of the creation of some kind of central state and then the, as it were, idealistic imposition of a perfect shari'at machine, as cynically put forward by the modernists with their rhetoric, while all the time bound to the anthropology of kafir governance.

Jihad as soon as realistically possible, by raid, in order to provide funds, until it is by battles, is the goal. The model is our Master, the Best of Creation, may Allah bless him and grant him peace, who, when he himself was not present on the raid, would appoint a number of his Companions to be in charge of the army and the raiders. They divided the ghanima on the spot, and thus the two offices became joined. It is for the Imam to do this. The division of fay' was known during the lifetime of the Messenger, may Allah bless him and grant him peace.

There is no doubt that you will hear people denounce these very matters discussed in this text and lie by using abrogated ayats and commands, deliberately to prevent the defeat of their kafir paymasters, and that particularly in the so-called faculties of Islamic law and learning in the kafir universities. All the matters outlined here are under the Sunna and the Salaf's actions. Texts on the subjects abound. As for the Jizya and the kharaj, for which there is evidence above, the Messenger, may Allah bless him and grant him peace, when he made peace with the Ukaydir Duma and the people of Bahrain, appointed al-'Ala' ibn al-Hadrami as Amir over them after having the Jizya and kharaj assessed.

As for the three types of disciplinary wars examined above - leaving Islam, brigands and rebels - the first two occurred during the lifetime of the Messenger, may Allah bless him and grant him peace. On one occasion, he cut off the hands and feet of some robbers and had them blinded, then left in the sun to die. The criminal had professed Islam to the Messenger, may Allah bless him and grant him peace, gone with his camel-herder into the desert saying that they wanted to rest, they then killed the herder and drove off the camels. The narrator of the hadith (*Sahih* of Bukhari: *Kitab ad-Diyat*) adds, "What could be worse than what these people did?

They left Islam, committed murder and stole."

Thus the means and the methods of Jihad and the execution of the hadd punishments for crimes are matters demanding the immediate application by the Muslims as the commencement of their imposition of law and order over the anarchy, decadence and manifest moral weakness of the kuffar. Now, while there is clear evidence that the current rulers over the Muslims are puppets and lackeys of the kuffar, and while a simple perusal of the laws, which it is obligatory that they uphold, reveals that they do not do so and that they impose laws which go against the ordinances of Allah and His Messenger, may Allah bless him and grant him peace, we caution the active Muslim not to be led by a trap deliberately set. If they 'aim' at the leaders and the structuralist state they will be defeated and humiliated at the present time, given the pyramidic and pharaonic tower of structuralist statism, the jewish defence system against defeat.

It is incumbent nevertheless not to fall into despair, nor to desist, nor to feel that only the suicide mission is of avail. If you are being attacked by a machine-gunner who from the vantage point of a tower can seek and destroy the Muslims, then every time you emerge to fire on him you are killed, surely the strategy of the situation demands not to take aim at the gunner but rather to destroy his vantage point, the tower from which he operates. And is this not what we have been presenting to you in this work - an indication that the monetary system is the means by which all these kafir rulers maintain their stranglehold on the Muslim Umma and the heartland of our beloved Arab brothers?

A wide-ranging and well-targetted series of raids will be the first stage of this fighting. It will lead in significant areas and indeed countries to the emergence of national military support from Islamically educated officers who will lead their men from shame and disgrace at the hands of the kuffar to victory and success as promised in the Qur'an. If bank raids and hostage-taking will constitute the first phase of the battle there is no doubt that the lands released from tyranny will immediately repudiate the false debt system and its obligations, which has brought nothing but humiliation to the muslim people and this will form the middle stage of the operation. The third stage is the establishment of Dar al-Islam in all its intellectual glory and the re-establishment of justice and equity and sanity where before there ruled decadence and madness. This was the Islamic achievement of the Madina of the Messenger, may Allah bless him and grant him peace, and of the Salaf. This was the glorious social justice of the Murabitun of Andalusia and its renowned fuqaha', Ibn Rushd al-Kabir, protector of the method of Madina, Abu Bakr ibn al-'Arabi, Ibn Juzayy, and so on.

Simultaneity of attack from Jakarta to the West at these same targets of the banking entity and its personnel will result in the desperation of the kuffar, the spreading thin of their forces, the dislocation of their structuralist communication system and the end of their monetary system. In all this, unity of the Muslims is essential. To this end it is vital that there is common agreement that the matter be firmly based on the Book and the Sunna. There can be no percolation through modernist/mu'tazila language, and there must be a firm rejection of a vocabulary and dialectic of the jews which talks of 'solidarity with human rights movements and the oppressed everywhere'. The problems of the kuffar are theirs, not ours. May they increase. We, for our part, must raise high the banner of Islam for the people, make the call clear that it may be answered by our own forces, and those kuffar who see the truth and come into Islam. Obedience to local Amirs is essential and deviation should be strictly punished. Thus, ideologically we must take a strong Salafi position and the clearest and most powerful position is that 'Umari Islam which is based on 'Amal - on action and behaviour. It is by a return to the source that the matter will succeed.

The source is our Master, Muhammad, may Allah bless him and grant him peace: there is the first Tabaqat. The Second Tabaqat is the Sahaba. The Third Tabaqat is the Tabi'un. The Fourth Tabaqat is in the Imam of Dar al-Hijra, Malik ibn Anas. The Fifth Tabaqat is: in the Hijaz, Ibn Majishun; in 'Iraq, Ibn Mubarak; in Misr, Ibn Hakim; in Andalus, Ibn Bashir. From these great Imams is a clear unbroken practice of activist Islam with the Maghrib entering the affair in the next Tabaqat with Sahnun. And so on across the whole Umma can be traced an unbroken line of teachers up until this century. It is important that the teaching of Madina return to Madina as it was before, and with that we will see an end to the domination of the Hijaz by foreign and enemy military enclaves, an end to a second resident deen in the land of the Arabs, and the beginning of the purification of the Umma from the source. When non-Muslims and jews are again paying the Jizya and are relegated to the rank of the Ahl adh-Dhimma then the Haramayn will be safe from mushrik activity, pseudo-sufism, kafir spies and subversive military attacks against the Haramayn. There is no way an Islamic society would permit an uprising in the most Inviolable Place. Such an event is an ineradicable disgrace which removes from those who permitted it their legitimate right to claim they are its protectors.

The fact of petro-chemical industrial activity does not license the existence of kafir enclaves under their own laws on the Arabian peninsula. "No two deens in the land of the Arabs." But again it is clear that attack will not succeed until it is directed against that edifice which supports and gives power to the - in fact - utterly weak and demoralised forces of kufr.

The final part of this brief analysis consists of an examination of the Mother Ayat, the great Ayat as-Sayf, and its commentaries by the great among the honoured mufassirun and on which there is not the slightest shadow of doubt or disagreement within this blessed Umma. May Allah give us inspiration by it and protection from all these shayatin who count on the ignorance of men by quoting ayats sent down on the Muslims in Makka in the time of their weakness, when Allah encouraged them by giving them command only to do what they were capable of, when it is well-known that these blessed ayats have been abrogated by those majestic Madinan ayats which call to war and set war as the means and method of the spread, establishment and victory of Islam until it dominates the kuffar. In its beginning, there was no compulsion in the deen, and then Allah, in His Might and Majesty, and by His sublime warrior Messenger, may Allah bless him and grant him peace, put power into the hands of the Muslims and compulsion was theirs, victory was theirs and the glorious establishment of the just society was theirs and that was Madina the Illuminated, may Allah protect it and return its primal teaching to its source. Amin.

THE AYAT OF THE SWORD

> So if you meet the kuffar, then a striking of necks, until, when you have done a lot of killing amongst them, then to tying the bonds tightly; then, afterwards, either graciousness or a ransom until the war lays down its burdens. That (is the ordinance). And if Allah willed He could have punished them (without you); but (thus it is) that He may try some of you by means of others; and those who are killed in the way of Allah, He will not let their actions be lost. (47:4)

Ibn Juzayy says in his *Ahkam, Tashil at-Tanzil*:

> "then a striking of necks": the root of it is to hit the necks with a hitting. The verb is left out, and the verbal noun stands in its place, and the meaning is "kill them". But He expressed this by the phrase "striking of necks" as this is the most usual way of killing.
>
> "until, when you have done a lot of killing amongst them": that is, you defeat them, and this word *ithkhan* means a lot of killing, and taking prisoners.

"Then to tying the bonds tightly": is an expression for taking people as prisoners.

"Then, afterwards, either graciousness or ransom": graciousness means setting free, and ransoming is releasing the prisoners for money - and they are both acceptable.

The method of Malik is that the Imam has the choice of five options regarding prisoners:

1. Graciousness.
2. Ransoming.
3. Killing.
4. Making them slaves.
5. Applying the Jizya.

It is also said that graciousness and ransoming are not acceptable because the ayat is abrogated by Allah's words: "Kill the mushrikun" so that because of this only killing them is acceptable. But the correct view is that the ayat's judgments are valid.

"Until the war lays down its burdens": linguistically 'burdens' means 'weights' and the meaning is "until its weights vanish and disappear". The weights are the instruments of war. It has also been said that the burdens are wrong actions because in war there has to be wrong action on one of the two sides. There is difference of opinion as to what the actual meaning his - it has been said that it means "until everybody becomes Muslim", at which point war will put down its burdens, and it has been said that it means "until you kill them and you get victory over them", and it has also been said "until 'Isa ibn Maryam comes down."

Ibn 'Atiyya said that the outward meaning of the expression is that it is a metaphor by which is meant the continuance of the situation forever just as you might say, "I am going to do that until the Day of Rising."

"That": what is understood is "the situation is that" or "that is the situation."

"And if Allah had wanted He could have punished them": and the meaning is, "if Allah had wanted He would have destroyed the kuffar with a torment from Him, but He wanted, may He be exalted, to test the muminun, and to try some people by means of others.

****

Abu Bakr ibn al-'Arabi says in his *Ahkam:*

Regarding this ayat there are nine points.

1. The first point is about grammar. "A striking of necks" is the verbal noun, with the meaning of the verb, that is, strike their necks, as if you were saying "go for a striking of necks" and the same thing applies to Allah's words "then afterwards either graciousness or a ransom", meaning *do* that.

2. His word, *kafaru*. There are two views on this:

    a) that they are the mushrikun, which is what Ibn 'Abbas said.
    b) it is everybody that has no treaty (*'ahd*) and contracted protection (*dhimma*), and this (second view) is the correct one because the ayat is general.

3. There are two views about Allah's words "a striking of necks":

    a) that is means fighting, which is what as-Suddi said.
    b) that is means killing prisoners without further ado. The most obvious meaning is that it is about fighting, which is "meeting", but we can also take the meaning of killing a prisoner without further ado because of the Messenger doing it, may Allah bless him and grant him peace, and ordering it to be done.

4. Allah's words "until, when you have done a lot of killing amongst them, then to tying the bonds tightly". The meaning is to kill them, until when a lot of that has happened and you have taken whoever is left behind, then tie them up firmly. After that you can either be gracious to them by letting them go for nothing, or you can ransom them, which is the fifth point.

5. As the Messenger, may Allah bless him and grant him peace, did with Abu 'Azza and Thumama. Muqatil said, "It is freeing", and Ibn Wahb and Ibn al-Qasim related the same from Malik.

6. The words "until the war lays down its burdens", mean its weights, and by it He is expressing weapons, because of their weight when being carried. There are three views about this:

> a) that it means until they believe and kufr goes, which is what al-Farra' said.
> b) until all creation becomes Muslim, which is what al-Kalbi said.
> c) until 'Isa ibn Maryam comes down, which is what Mujahid said.

7. People disagree about whether this ayat has been abrogated, or whether its judgments apply. It has been said that it is abrogated by Allah's words, "kill the mushrikun wherever you find them", which is what as-Suddi said.

The second view is that it is abrogated as far as pagans are concerned because you cannot make treaties with them, and it has also been said that its judgments are applicable right across the board, which is what ad-Dahhak said.

The third view is that its judgments are valid after there has been a lot of killing, which is what Sa'id ibn az-Zubayr said, because of Allah's words, "It is not for any Messenger to have any prisoners until he has done a lot of killing on the earth."

The correct view is that its judgments are valid as regards the command to fight, according to what we have made clear.

8. Regarding re-examination of the ayat.

Know, may Allah give you success, that this ayat is one of the Mother Ayats and one of those which contain judgments in which Allah ordered fighting and stated clearly how it should be, as He stated clearly in His words, "Strike above their necks, and strike from them every fingertip," according to what has gone before in *Surat al-Anfal*.

If a Muslim is in a position to deliver a blow to the neck of a kafir, then he should finish him off. Iif he gets the chance to hit his hand with which he defends himself and which he uses to fight other people, then he should do that. If the only thing he can do is to hit his horse which he uses to get where he wants to go (then he should do so). Thus the kafir is either on foot like the Muslim or on foot beneath him - because if the kafir is above him then he wants to bring him down to his level, and if he is the same as him, then he wants to bring him down lower. The target is his enemy's life, and the outcome is that the word of Allah is highest.

That is because when Allah first ordered fighting

knowing that it would reach the point of much bloodshed and victory, He made clear the judgments regarding victory such as tying the bonds firmly, and at that point the Muslims have the choice of graciousness or ransom. That is what ash-Shafi'i said.

Abu Hanifa said that they only have the choice of killing or taking slaves, because in his opinion this ayat is abrogated.

Abu Bakr says that the correct view is that its judgments are valid because the conditions of abrogation are not fulfilled in this ayat, because of the contradiction that would occur, because the first part of the ayat links to the second part, and because His words, "If you meet them in war, then use them to frighten those who come after, that hopefully they will remember."

There is no convincing argument in it (for abrogation) because scaring them off can be done by graciousness, ransom, or killing, because the halter of shame at being set free for nothing weighs heavily on the necks of men, and takes away their self-esteem, and ransoming depletes their wealth, and al-'Abbas was under the weight of the ransom of Badr until the Messenger, may Allah bless him and grant him peace, paid it for him.

As for Allah's words "kill the mushrikun wherever you find them", He has also said, "and besiege them" and He ordered that they be taken as well as killed. And if it is said that He ordered that they be taken *in order* to be killed, then we say *or* to be freed, or to be ransomed, all of which Allah supports.

Muslim related that the Messenger, may Allah bless him and grant him peace, took a slavegirl from Salama ibn al-Akwa' and ransomed her in return for a number of Muslims, and a group of Makkans came down on the Messenger, may Allah bless him and grant him peace, and he took them prisoner, and freed them for nothing. He also set free the war prisoners of the Hawazin, and killed an-Nadr ibn al-Harith without further ado.

As for His saying "until the war lays down its burdens", it means, according to one group of people "until war lays down its wrong actions", that is, that everybody becomes Muslim, and no kafir remains, which ends up meaning "until there is no more Jihad," which will not be until the Day of Judgment, because of the saying of the Messenger, may Allah bless him and grant him peace, "Horses have good tied up in their forelocks until the Day of Judgment", that is, reward and booty (ghanima).

Those who mention the coming down of 'Isa ibn Maryam do so because of what is related that when he comes down there will be no kafir left from among the People of the Book, and no Jizya. It is that those who have no Book will remain and that Jizya will not be accepted from them according to the most correct of the two views, which we have made clear in the Book of Hadith.

9. Final word.

Al-Hasan and 'Ata' said that there is, grammatically speaking, a "bringing forward" and a "putting back" because the meaning is "so a striking of necks until war lays down its burdens. And when you have done a lot of killing, then to tying bonds tightly"; and the Imam does not have the option of killing a prisoner.

****

In the tafsir of al-Qurtubi we find:

Regarding this there are four points:

1. Is Allah's word "If you meet those who do kufr then a striking of necks". Having distinguished between the two groups of people (in a previous ayat) He orders Jihad against the kuffar.

Ibn 'Abbas said that the kuffar are the mushrikun who worship idols. It has also been said anyone who goes against the Deen of Islam whether a mushrik or a person of the Book, if he is not someone under treaty of dhimma.

Al-Mawardi mentioned this and Ibn al-'Arabi chose it and said it is the correct view because of the general nature of the ayat.

The "striking of necks" is the verbal noun, that is, using the order "strike necks" as Hajjaj said, that is "strike the necks!" He especially mentioned necks because that is the usual way in which killing is done. It has also been said that it is the *nasb* (accusative) for incitement. Abu 'Ubayda said that it is like when you say "O patience!"

It is also said that what is said is "seek a striking of necks". He said, "then a striking of necks" and He did not say "then kill them", because in the use of the expression "striking of necks" is a roughness and a force which the word killing does not have, because of how it depicts killing in its ugliest form which is cutting into the neck and causing the limb which is the head of the body, its highest point and the noblest of the limbs, to fly off.

2. Allah the Exalted saying "until when you have done a lot of killing amongst them": We have already seen the words of Allah in *Surat al-Anfal* "until he does a lot of killing on the earth."

"Then tie bonds tightly": that is, when you take them prisoner.

"Then, afterwards, either graciousness" (towards them by setting them free without a ransom) "or a ransom" and He did not mention killing here, making do with what has already been said previously about killing.

It is related from one of them that he said, "I was standing next to al-Hajjaj when the prisoners of the friends of 'Abd ar-Rahman ibn al-Ashraf were brought to him. There were 4,800 of them, and he killed some 3,000 of them until a man from Kinda came up to him and said, "O Hajjaj, may Allah not reward you with good for your going against the

Sunna and generosity." He said, "Why is that?" He replied, "Because Allah the Exalted said, 'if you meet the kuffar....or a ransom' about those who did not believe. And by Allah, you have neither been gracious nor have you ransomed, and your poet, describing the noble qualities of character of his people said, 'and we do not kill prisoners but we release them' when the weight of financial obligations, that is, ransom, weighs too heavily on their necks." And al-Hajjaj said, "Huh! All those corpses! Was there not one among them who could have said such good words? Let the rest of them go!" And on that day the rest of the prisoners, who were nearly 2,000, were freed because of what that man said.

(Al-Qurtubi then examines five different positions on the matter of abrogation. He concludes this with his own position:)

That the ayat is not abrogated, that its judgments are sound and that the Imam has the choice of every situation, which is what 'Ali ibn Abi Talha related from Ibn 'Abbas and what many 'ulama', among them Ibn 'Umar and al-Hasan and 'Ata' said, and it is the madh-hab of Malik and ash-Shafi'i and ath-Thawri and al-Awza'i and Abu 'Ubayd and others, and it is the best view to take because the Messenger of Allah, may Allah bless him and grant him peace, and the Khulafa' ar-Rashidun did all of these things. The Messenger, may Allah bless him and grant him peace, killed 'Uqba ibn Abi Mu'ayt and an-Nadr ibn al-Harith without further ado on the day of Badr, and he ransomed the rest of the prisoners of Badr. He set free Thumama ibn Uthal al-Hanafi while he was a prisoner in his hands, and he took a slavegirl from Salama ibn al-'Akwa and by her ransomed a number of Muslims. A group of Makkans came down on the Messenger, may Allah bless him and grant him peace, and he captured them and set them free and he also set free the war prisoners of the Hawazin.

All of this is confirmed by accurate Hadith, all of which have been mentioned in the tafsir of *Surat al-Anfal* and elsewhere as well.

An-Nahhas said this is based on the judgments of the two ayats being acted upon and valid, and this is what al-Hasan said, because abrogation can only be for something definite. So if it is possible to act according to the two ayats, then it is meaningless to say it is abrogated, since it is acceptable that it is an act of worship to kill the kuffar when we meet them. If prisoners are taken it is acceptable to kill them or make them slaves or ransom them, or just set them free, according to what is of most benefit to the Muslims.

As to Allah's saying "until the war puts down its burdens", Mujahid and Ibn Jubayr say this is when 'Isa ibn Maryam comes out. Also from Mujahid is that it means "until there is no other Deen than the Deen of Islam when every jew and Christian and those of other groups become Muslim and the sheep are safe from the jackals. Al-Hasan, al-Kalbi, al-Farra' and al-Kisa'i say the same. Al-Kisa'i says "until all creation becomes muslim." Al-Farra' says "until Islam prevails over every other religion". Al-Hasan says "until they worship only Allah."

∗∗

In the tafsir *Ruh al-Ma'ani* by Abu'l-Fadl al-Baghdadi in his commentary on this ayat, confirming all that is stated above and enlarging on it, he says:

> Ahmad (ibn Hanbal), an-Nasa'i and others relate that Salama ibn Nufayl said: "Once while I was sitting with the Messenger of Allah, may Allah bless him and grant him peace, a man came and said, 'O Messenger of Allah, the horses have been let go, the weapons have been put down and some people claim that there is no jihad now, and that war has laid down its burdens.' The Messenger of Allah, may Allah bless him and grant him peace, said, 'They are lying. For now war has come and there will always be a group of my Umma in Jihad in the way of Allah who will not be harmed by those who oppose them. And Allah the Exalted will make the hearts of some people turn away in order to give them (the Muslims) provision from them. And you will be fighting until the Hour comes, and horses will always have good tied up in their forelocks until the

Hour comes and war will not put down its burdens until Yajuj and Majuj come out."

****

And to conclude the matter here is Ibn Juzayy in his *Tas-hil at-Tanzil* commenting on the ayat that speaks of Allah and His Messenger, may Allah bless him and grant him peace, declaring war on usury:

> "And if you do not, be warned of war": If you do not stop usury, war will be made on you. And be warned means, read with the *madda*, to make it known to others than yourselves. When it was sent down, Thaqif said, "We cannot endure a war with Allah and His Messenger."

※ ※ ※ ※ ※ ※ ※ ※ ※ ※

The blessings of Allah and peace on the unlettered Messenger Muhammad, on his family and all his Companions. Amin.

※ ※ ※ ※ ※ ※ ※ ※ ※ ※